Introduction: Television and Thinking People

Douglass Cater

In January, 1949, only 2.3 percent of American homes had the box with the cathode-ray tube. Five years later, more than half of our homes had been penetrated by television. Today, 97 percent have one or more sets—a distribution roughly matching that of indoor plumbing. With American TV approaching its quarter-century anniversary as a household phenomenon, one might think we would have devoted serious attention by now to the effects of this medium on our culture, our society, our lives. Certainly we might expect at this point to be trying to articulate the consequences of the even more enveloping telecommunications environment which lies ahead. Yet, as the prescient Mr. Marconi predicted a long time ago, telecommunications has quickly become part of the "almost unnoticed working equipment of civilization."

Why unnoticed? What has prevented thinking people from applying their critical faculties to this medium, which reaches greater masses than all the other mass media combined (nearly twice as many sets in U.S. homes as the total daily circulation of newspapers)? Why haven't more of our talented scholars been attracted to the study of this new environment? Why do the media themselves devote so little attention to serious television analysis and criticism? Why have our foundations provided only very limited resources for the study of communications, which is as fundamental to society as education, health, or our physical environment?

I would suggest three speculative reasons for these failures. In the first place, scientific evidence suggests that thinking people at least those over the age of twenty-five—are left-brained in development. They rely predominantly on the left hemisphere, which controls sequential, analytical tasks based on

---

Douglass Cater is Director of the Aspen Institute Program on Communications and Society.

the use of propositional thought. TV, we are informed, appeals mainly to the right hemisphere of the brain, which controls appositional thought.

Scientists and theologians alike have pondered how the two halves of the brain relate—whether they ignore, inhibit, cooperate, compete, or simply take turns at the control center. But whole cultures seem to show preference for one or the other mode of thought, and thinking people of the Western world have up until now plighted their troth with propositional thought. But after five centuries of slowly acquired sophistication in distinguishing the truth from the trickery transmitted by Mr. Gutenberg's invention, we now find ourselves having to master the non-linear logic created by a steady bombardment of sights and sounds on our senses. The thinking person is apt to be somewhat bewildered by the telly and to regard it in the same way a back-sliding prohibitionist regards hard liquor—as something to be indulged in with a sense of guilt. The "educated viewer," according to Robert T. Bower's analysis of viewing habits, has learned to live with ambivalence: Although he may be scornful of commercial TV fare, "he watches the set (by his own admission) as much as others during the evening and weekend hours . . . even when he had a clear choice between an information program and some standard entertainment fare, he was just as apt as others to choose the latter."[1]

The peculiar structure of the American television industry is a second reason why the thinking person refuses to think seriously about the medium. The broadcast industry is based on a marketplace unlike any other in our private enterprise economy. It offers its product "free" to the consumer and depends on advertising to supply, by latest count, gross annual revenues of $4.5 billion. As a result, commercial TV's prime allegiance is to the merchant, not the viewer. To attract the advertising dollar, the programmer seeks to capture the dominant share of the viewers and to hold them unblinking for the longest period of time. Everything else is subordinated to this dogged pursuit of mankind in the mass. A program attracting many millions is deemed a failure and discarded if it happens to be scheduled opposite a program attracting even more millions.

Within this iron regime of dollars and ratings, a few ghettos of do-goodism exist. Network news and documentaries as well as occasional dramas of exceptional quality reveal an upward striving in television (dismissed by some cynics as tithing to the Federal regulators). But these programs fare poorly in the competition for television's most precious commodity—time. A former network news chief has remarked, "They don't mind how much money and talent we devote to producing documentaries so long as we don't ask for prime time evening hours to show them." Even the daylight hours have to be tightly rationed when the marathon melodramas of Washington start competing with the soap operas of Hollywood.

Thinking people do not know how to cope with a system whose economic laws, they are led to believe, are immutable. Any suggestions they may have for TV's betterment are characterized as naive, elitist, and offensive to the First Amendment. The proper posture is to sit back and be thankful when broadcast officialdom chooses to violate its own laws and reveal fleetingly what a fantastic instrument of communication television can be.

A third reason why thinking people have difficulty coming to grips with television is that we have yet to develop satisfactory measures with which to gauge this environmental phenomenon. Consider, as an example, the Surgeon General's inquiry into televised violence and its effect on the behavior of children. Conducted over three years at a cost of $1.8 million, and based on twenty-three separate laboratory and field studies, this was the most far-reaching probe to date into the social consequences of television. In its final report the Surgeon General's Committee could acknowledge only "preliminary and tentative" evidence of a causal relationship between TV violence and aggression in children.

For an industry dedicated to the proposition that thirty-second commercials can change a viewer's buying behavior, it would be folly to ignore this warning about the not-so-subliminal effects of its program content. But these studies, mostly gauging immediate response to brief TV exposure, could not adequately measure the impact of the total phenomenon—the experience of the child who spends up to six hours a day, year in and year out, before the set. This is what makes television different from reading books or going to the movies.

How to measure the long-term, less flamboyant effects of the environment created by television? In 1938, E.B. White witnessed a TV demonstration and wrote, "A door closing, heard over the air, a face contorted seen in a panel of light, these will emerge as the real and the true. And when we bang the door of our own cell or look into another's face, the impression will be of mere artifice." Now, a third of a century later, comes Tony Schwartz to carry the speculation further.[2] Mr. Schwartz' insights have peculiar power because he was the creator of the ill-famed political commercial in 1964 showing a child innocently picking daisy petals as a countdown for a hydrogen bomb blast. Though there was no mention of the presidential candidate against whom the message was aimed, the effect of the commercial was so unnerving that it was withdrawn by its sponsors after a single showing. Schwartz appears to know whereof he theorizes.

Gutenberg man, he writes, lived by a communication system requiring the laborious coding of thought into words and then the equally laborious decoding by the receiver—akin to the loading, shipping and unloading of a railway freight car. Electronic man dispenses with this, communicating experience without the need of symbolic transformations. What the viewer's brain gets is a mosaic of myriad dots of light and vibrations of sound which are stored and recalled at high speed. Amid this electronic bombardment, Schwartz speculates, a barrier has been crossed akin to the supersonic sound barrier, or, in his image, the 90-mile-an-hour barrier when a motorcycle racer must turn *into* rather than *out with* a skid: "... in communicating at electronic speed we no longer direct information into an audience but try to evoke stored information out of them in a patterned way."

The function of the electronic communicator, according to Schwartz, "is to achieve a state of resonance with the person receiving visual and auditory stimuli." The Gutenberg communicator—for the past five hundred years patiently transmitting experience line by line, usually left to right, down the printed page—is no longer relevant. TV man has become conditioned to a total communication environment, to constant stimuli which he shares with everyone else in society and to which he is conditioned to respond instantly. Schwartz believes that the totality and instantaneousness of television, more than its particular program content, contributes to violence in society.

His premises lead him to the shattering conclusion that "truth is a print ethic, not a standard for ethical behavior in electronic communication." We must now be concerned not with Gutenberg-based concepts of truth but with the "effects" of electronic communication: "A whole new set of questions must be asked, and a whole new theory of communications must be formulated."

Without going all the way with Schwartz, we clearly need to examine TV's effects more diligently. What, for example, is television doing to the institutions and forms and rituals of our democracy? In 1968, sitting in Washington, I watched TV coverage of the disastrous Democratic Convention in Chicago. At one moment, all hell broke loose in the area where the Wisconsin delegation was seated. Immediately, the TV cameras zoomed in and reporters rushed there with walkie-talkies. In an instant, the whole viewing nation knew the cause of the trouble, while Speaker Carl Albert, presiding over the convention, didn't know. Yet Albert was the one who had to decide what to do about the problem. In microcosm, one witnessed how leadership can be hustled by such a formidable communications system.

Politicians are struggling to learn the grammar of TV communication and to master the body English so different from that of the stump speech. TV has markedly influenced the winnowing process by which some politicians are sorted out as prospects for higher office and others are not. TV has contributed to abbreviation of the political dialogue and even changed the ground rules by which candidates map their campaign itineraries.

TV has nurtured widespread illusions about recreating a Greek marketplace of direct democracy. When citizens can see and hear what they believe to be the actuality, why should they rely on intermediating institutions to make the decisions for them? When political leaders can reach directly to their constituents without the help of a political party, why should they not opt for "the people's" mandate rather than "the party's"? Recent Presidents and Presidential candidates have been notably affected by this line of reasoning. It

Television as a Social Force:

New Approaches to TV Criticism

Douglass Cater Editor, Aspen Series on
Communications and Society

Richard Adler Project Editor, TV Workshop

Sponsored by the

Aspen Institute on Communications

and Society

The Praeger Special Studies program—
utilizing the most modern and efficient book
production techniques and a selective
worldwide distribution network—makes
available to the academic, government, and
business communities significant, timely
research in U.S. and international economic, social, and political development.

Television as a Social Force:

New Approaches to TV Criticism

Praeger Publishers   New York   Washington   London

PRAEGER SPECIAL STUDIES IN U.S. ECONOMIC, SOCIAL, AND POLITICAL ISSUES

Library of Congress Cataloging in Publication Data
Main entry under title:

Television as a Social Force: New Approaches to TV Criticism.

(Praeger special studies in U.S. economic, social, and political issues)
Includes index.
1. Television criticism—Addresses, essays, lectures. 2. Television broad-
casting—Social aspects—United States—Addresses, essays, lectures. I. Adler,
Richard. II. Aspen Institute Program on Communications and Society.
PN1992.8.C7A6   301.16'2   75-6835
ISBN 0-915436-02-7 Paperback
ISBN 0-275-01190-9 Cloth

*The essays in this volume are first products of the Aspen Program's
Workshop on Television whose purpose is to stimulate fresh examination
of TV's impact on society and to persuade leading humanists to think
about this pervasive medium. Quotations appearing between the essays
come from discussions at the Aspen Conference in August, 1974, which
reviewed the preliminary essay drafts. Participants are listed in the
appendix. The Workshop has received support from the National Endowment for the Humanities and the John and Mary R. Markle Foundation.*

PRAEGER PUBLISHERS
111 Fourth Avenue, New York, N.Y. 10003, U.S.A.
5, Cromwell Place, London SW7 2JL, England

ASPEN INSTITUTE PROGRAM ON COMMUNICATIONS & SOCIETY
360 Bryant Street
Palo Alto, CA 94301

exposes an ancient vulnerability of our republic in which so much political lip service is paid to the notion that public opinion should rule everything.

How can democracy be strengthened within the environment of television? Why, in an age of abundant communication, has there been a continuing decline in voter participation? Michael Robinson, a political scientist, cites surveys which indicate that heavy TV viewers are more apt than light viewers to be turned off by politics.[3] He speculates that the more dependent an individual becomes on TV as his principal source of information, the more likely he is to feel that he cannot understand or affect the political process. TV, unlike newspapers, reaches many who are not motivated to seek information about public affairs and these "inadvertent" audiences, in Robinson's view, are frequently confused and alienated by what they see. Such a proposition runs directly counter to the usual reformist instinct to prescribe more programming to overcome voter apathy. Professor Robinson's speculations need to be probed more deeply.

What will be the future? George Orwell had a vision of a time—less than a decade away—when the communications environment would be employed for the enslavement rather than the enlightenment of mankind. Orwell called his system "Big Brother." For the present anyway, we can conceive of a less ominous communications future with MOTHER, which is the acronym for "Multiple Output Telecommunication Home End Resources."

What will be the technical characteristics of MOTHER? First, she will offer infinitely more channels—via microwave, satellite, cable, laser beam—than the present broadcast spectrum provides. There will also be greater capacity crammed within each channel—more information "bits" per gigahertz—so that one can simultaneously watch a program and receive a newspaper print-out on the same channel.

A life-sized MOTHER, giving the illusion of three dimensions, will be able to narrowcast to neighborhoods or other focused constituencies. She will be "interactive," permitting us to talk back to our television set by means of a digital device on the console. Recording and replay equipment, already being marketed, will liberate us from the tyranny of the broadcast schedule, and computer hookup and stop-frame control will bring the Library of Congress and other Gutenberg treasuries into our living room.

Finally, via the satellite, MOTHER will offer world-wide programming in what the communications experts artfully call "real time" (even if real time means that Mohammed Ali must fight at 4:00 A.M. in Zaire in order to suit the prime time of New Yorkers). Although MOTHER will be able to beam broadcasts from the People's Republic of China directly to a household in the U.S. and vice versa, she may face political barriers.

Until recently, prophets foresaw that the cable and other technological advances would transform television from a wholesale to a retail enterprise, directly offering the consumer a genuine diversity of choice. The "television of abundance" would bring not just greater variety of programs but also new concepts of programming—continuing education, health delivery, community services. Television would become a participatory instrument of communication rather than a one-way flow.

Today, these visions are not so bright. Some critics now glumly predict that the new technology will suffer the fate of the supersonic transport. Others expect the technology to be developed, but it will serve strictly commercial rather than social purposes. Computer may be talking to computer by cable and satellite, but householders will still be watching "I Love Lucy" on their TV sets.

My own expectation is that the next decade or two will radically alter America's communications. The important issue is whether it will be for better or for worse. If it is to be "for better," we must give more critical attention to TV than we have given in the past. Too much critical time has been wasted worrying about the worst of television. More attention should be paid to the best, not simply laudatory attention but a systematic examination of style and technique and message. Criticism should also extend its reach beyond the intellectual elite into elementary and secondary schools, where children can be stimulated to think about the medium which so dominates their waking hours. We must endeavor to raise the viewers' capacity to distinguish truth from sophistry, or at least their awareness, in Schwartz's vocabulary, of the "resonance" being evoked from them.

There needs to be more widespread analysis and debate of the potential for new media and for new forms within the media. Could an electronic box office for pay programming repeal the iron laws governing "free" commercial television? How do we move beyond the limits of present broadcasting toward broader social purposes for television? In an era when life-long learning has become essential to prevent human obsolescence, television surely has a role to play. And television might regularly deliver some types of health service now that the doctor is seldom making house-calls. Health and education are gargantuan national enterprises costing upwards of $200 billion annually. Yet only paltry sums are being invested for research and demonstration to develop TV's capacity to enrich and extend them.

Finally, we must move beyond our preoccupation with the production and transmission processes in media communication. An equally important question is what gets through? The editors of *Scientific American* report that man's visual system has more than a million channels, capable of transmitting instantly 10^7 bits of information to the brain. Yet the brain has the capacity for receiving only twenty-seven bits of information per second. These are the raw statistics of communication within the human anatomy. They lead Sir John Eccles, the Nobel Prize-winning physiologist, to believe that the most important frontier of brain research involves the study of inhibition—our capacity to censor stimuli in order to prevent overload. Sir John makes the comparison: "It's like sculpture. What you cut away from the block of stone produces the statue."

Our journalists, both on TV and in print, pledge fealty to the proposition that society thrives by the communication of great gobs of unvarnished truth. Our law courts make us swear to tell "the truth, the whole truth, and nothing but the truth." Yet we only dimly understand how, in an all-enveloping information environment, man chisels his little statues of perceived reality. As we approach a time when communication threatens to fission like the atom, we need to delve more deeply into these mysteries.

Looking far ahead, Robert Jastrow, Director of the Goddard Institute of Space Studies, foresees a fifth communications revolution more radical even than the previous four revolutions of speech, writing, printing, and radio. "In the long term, the new satellites will provide a nervous system for mankind, knitting the members of our species into a global society," Jastrow predicts and compares this to that change in the history of life several billion years ago when multicellular animals evolved out of more primitive organisms.

Before such an awesome prospect, thinking people may feel overwhelmed. Or else we can screw up our courage, ask the fundamental questions, and make the critical choices to shape our destiny.

Footnotes

1.   *Robert T. Bower,* Television and the Public *(Holt, Rinehart and Winston, Inc., 1973).*

2.   *See his recent book* The Responsive Chord *(Anchor/Doubleday, 1973).*

3.   *See his essay, page 97.*

What we call entertainment—which suggests relaxation, filling up an idle hour, a kind of passive, neutral experience—is really a tremendously complicated experience that touches all kinds of hidden springs and relates to our personal experience, our past, and also to the society and our place in the society. . . . In shaping pictures of the world, it may in fact be performing a journalistic function. I can't prove it; it is simply my hunch . . . I think that politics on television has not been primarily in speeches, but in dramatic material. One of the fascinating things about television is the continual overlapping of everything. Drama is inevitably propaganda, it's politics, it's also merchandising. It is continually selling a way of life or pattern of consumption.

Erik Barnouw

Television
Shapes
the Soul

Michael Novak

For twenty-five years we have been immersed in a medium never before experienced on this earth. We can be forgiven if we do not yet understand all the ways in which this medium has altered us, particularly our inner selves: the perceiving, mythic, symbolic—and the judging, critical—parts of ourselves.

Media, like instruments, work "from the outside in." If you practice the craft of writing sedulously, you begin to think and perceive differently. If you run for twenty minutes a day, your psyche is subtly transformed. If you work in an executive office, you begin to think like an executive. And if you watch six hours of television, on the average, every day . . . ?[1]

Innocent of psychological testing and sociological survey, I would like to present a humanist's analysis of what television seems to be doing to me, to my students, to my children, and, in general, to those I see around me (including those I see on television, in movies, in magazines, etc.). My method is beloved of philosophers, theologians, cultural critics: try to *perceive*, make *distinctions, coax into the light* elusive movements of consciousness. It goes without saying that others will have to verify the following observations; they are necessarily in the hypothetical mode, even if some of the hypotheses have a cogency that almost bites.

Two clusters of points may be made. The first, rather metaphysical, concerns the way television affects our way of perceiving and approaching reality. The second cluster concerns the way television inflicts a class bias on the world of our perceptions—the bias of a relatively small and special social class.[2]

Michael Novak has taught at Harvard, Stanford, and SUNY-Old Westbury; during 1973-4, he helped to establish a new Humanities Program at the Rockefeller Foundation. He is the author of several books including *Choosing Our King* (1974). Mr. Novak is currently serving as Chairman of the Aspen Institute's Workshop on Television.

9

1. Television and Reality

Television is a molder of the soul's geography. It builds up incrementally a psychic structure of expectations. It does so in much the same way that school lessons slowly, over the years, tutor the unformed mind and teach it "how to think." Television *might* tutor the mind, soul, and heart in other ways than the ways it does at present. But, to be concrete, we ought to keep in view the average night of programming on the major networks over the last decade or so—not so much the news or documentaries, not so much the discussions on public television or on Sundays, not so much the talk shows late at night, but rather the variety shows, comedies, and adventure shows that are the staples of prime-time viewing. From time to time we may allow our remarks to wander farther afield. But it is important to concentrate on the universe of prime-time major network programming; that is where the primary impact of television falls.

It is possible to isolate five or six ways in which television seems to affect those who watch it. Television series represent genres of artistic performance. They structure a viewer's way of perceiving, of making connections, and of following a story line. Try, for example, to bring to consciousness the difference between the experience of watching television and the experience of learning through reading, argument, the advice of elders, lectures in school, or other forms of structuring perception. The conventions of the various sorts of television series re-create different sorts of "worlds." These "worlds" raise questions—and, to some extent, illuminate certain features of experience that we notice in ourselves and around us as we watch.

(1) Suppose that you were a writer for a television show—an action-adventure, a situation comedy, even a variety show. You would want to be very careful to avoid "dead" spots, "wooden" lines, "excess" verbiage. Every line has a function, even a double or triple function. Characters move on camera briskly, every line counts, the scene shifts rapidly. In comedy, every other line should be a laugh-getter. Brevity is the soul of hits.

Television is a teacher of expectations; it speeds up the rhythm of attention. Any act in competition with television must approach the same pace; otherwise it will seem "slow." Even at an intellectual conference or seminar we now demand a swift rhythm of progressive movement; a leisurely, circular pace of rumination is perceived as less than a "good show."

(2) But not only the pace is fast. Change of scene and change of perspective are also fast. In a recent episode of *Kojak,* action in three or four parts of the city was kept moving along in alternating sequences of a minute or less. A "principle of association" was followed; some image in the last frames of one scene suggested a link to the first frames of the new scene. But one scene cut away from another very quickly.

The progression of a television show depends upon multiple

logics—two or three different threads are followed simultaneously. The viewer must figure out the connections between people, between chains of action, and between scenes. Many clues are *shown*, not *said*. The viewer must detect them.

The logic of such shows is not sequential in a single chain. One subject is raised, then cut, and another subject is picked up, then cut. Verbal links—"Meanwhile, on the other side of the city . . . "—are not supplied.

In teaching and in writing I notice that for students one may swiftly change the subject, shift the scene, drop a line of argument in order to pick it up later—and not lose the logic of development. Students understand such a performance readily. They have been prepared for it. The systems of teaching which I learned in my student days—careful and exact exegesis proceeding serially from point to point, the careful definition and elucidation of terms in an argument and the careful scrutiny of chains of inference, and the like—now meet a new form of resistance. There has always been resistance to mental discipline; one has only to read the notebooks of students from medieval universities to recognize this well-established tradition of resistance. But today the minds and affections of the brighter students are teeming with images, vicarious experiences, and indeed of actual travel and accomplishments. Their minds race ahead and around the flanks of lines of argument. "Dialectics" rather than "logic" or "exegesis" is the habit of mind they are most ready for. I say this neither in praise nor in blame; pedagogy must deal with this new datum, if it is new. What are its limits and its possibilities? What correctives are needed among students—and among teachers?

(3) The periodization of attention is also influenced by the format of television. For reasons of synchronized programming the ordinary television show is neatly divided into segments of approximately equal length, and each of these segments normally has its own dramatic rhythm so as to build to dramatic climax or sub-climax, with the appropriate degree of suspense or resolution. Just as over a period of time a professor develops an instinct for how much can be accomplished in a fifty-minute lecture, or a minister of religion develops a temporal pattern for his sermons, so also the timing of television shows tutors their audience to expect a certain rhythm of development. The competitive pressures of television, moreover, encourage producers to "pack" as much action, intensity, or (to speak generally) entertainment into each segment as possible. Hence, for example, the short, snappy gags of *Laugh-In* and the rapid-fire developments of police shows or westerns.

Character is as important to successful shows as action; audiences need to "identify" with the heroes of the show, whether dramatic or comic. Thus in some ways the leisure necessary to develop character may provide a counter-tendency to the need for melodramatic rapidity. Still, "fast-paced" and "laugh-packed" and other such descriptions express the sensibility that television both serves and reinforces.

(4) Television tutors the sensibilities of its audience in another way:

it can handle only a limited range of human emotions, perplexities, motivations, and situations. The structure of competitive television seems to require this limitation; it springs from a practiced estimation of the capacity of the audience. Critics sometimes argue that American novelists have a long tradition of inadequacy with respect to the creation of strong, complicated women and, correspondingly, much too simple and superficial a grasp of the depths and complexities of human love. It is, it is said, the more direct "masculine" emotions, as well as the relations of comradeship between men, that American artists celebrate best. If such critical judgments may be true of our greatest artists working in their chosen media, then, a fortiori, it is not putting down television to note that the range of human relations treated by artists on television is less than complete. The constraints under which television artists work are acute: the time available to them, the segmentation of this time, and the competitive pressures they face for intense dramatic activity. To develop a fully complicated set of motivations, internal conflicts, and inner contradictions requires time and sensitivity to nuance. The present structure of television makes these requirements very difficult to meet.

This point acquires fuller significance if we note the extent to which Americans depend upon television for their public sense of how other human beings behave in diverse situations. The extent of this dependence should be investigated. In particular, we ought to examine the effects of the growing segregation of Americans by age. It does not happen frequently nowadays that children grow up in a household shared by three generations, in a neighborhood where activities involve members of all generations, or in a social framework where generation-mixing activities are fairly common. I have many times been told by students (from suburban environments, in particular) that they have hardly ever, or never, had a serious conversation with adults. The social world of their parents did not include children. They spent little time with relatives, and that time was largely formal and distant. The high schools were large, "consolidated," and relatively impersonal. Their significant human exchanges were mostly with their peers. Their images of what adults do and how adults think and act were mainly supplied by various media, notably television and the cinema. The issue such comments raise is significant. Where *could* most Americans go to find dramatic models of adult behavior? In the eyes of young people does the public weight of what is seen on television count for more than what they see in their private world as a model for "how things are done"? Indeed, do adults themselves gain a sense of what counts as acceptable adult behavior from the public media?

If it turns out to be true that television (along with other media like magazines and the cinema) now constitutes a major source of guidance for behavior, to be placed in balance with what one learns from one's parents, from the churches, from one's local communities, and the like, then the range of dramatic materials on television has very serious consequences for the American psyche. While human behavior is to a remarkable extent diverse and variable, it tends to be "formed" and given shape by the attraction or the power of available imaginative materials: stories, models, symbols, images-in-action. The storehouse of imaginative materials available to each person provides a sort of repertoire. The impact of new models can be a powerful one, leading to "conversions," "liberations," or "new directions." The reservoir of acquired models exerts a strong influence both upon perception and upon response to unfamiliar models. If family and community ties weaken and if psychic development becomes somewhat more nuclearized or even atomized, the influence of television and other distant sources may well become increasingly powerful, moving, as it were, into something like a vacuum. Between the individual and the national source of image-making there will be little or no local resistance. The middle ground of the psyche, until recently thick and rich and resistant, will have become attenuated.

The point is not that television has reached the limit of its capacities, nor is it to compare the possibilities of television unfavorably with those of other media. It is, rather, to draw attention to television as it has been used in recent years and to the structures of attention that, by its presentations, it helps to shape.

The competitive pressures of programming may have brought about these limits. But it is possible that the nature of the medium itself precludes entering certain sorts of depths. Television may be excellent in some dimensions and merely whet the appetite in others.

(5) Television also seems to conceive of itself as a national medium. It does not favor the varieties of accent, speech patterns, and other differences of the culture of the United States. It favors a language which might be called "televisionese"—a neutral accent, pronunciation, and diction perhaps most closely approximated in California.

Since television arises in the field of "news" and daily entertainment, television values highly a kind of topicality, instant reflection of trends, and an effort to be "with it" and even "swinging." It values the "front edge" of attention, and it dreads being outrun by events. Accordingly, its product is perishable. It functions, in a way, as a guide to the latest gadgets and to the wonders of new technologies, or, as a direct contrary, to a kind of nostalgia for simpler ways in simpler times. Fashions of dress, automobiles, and explicitness "date" a series of shows. (Even the techniques used in taping shows may date them.)

Thus television functions as an instrument of the national, mobile culture. It does not reinforce the concrete ways of life of individual neighborhoods, towns, or subcultures. It shows the way things are done (or fantasized as being done) in "the big world." It is an organ of Hollywood and New York, not of Macon, Peoria, Salinas, or Buffalo.

I once watched television in a large hut in Tuy Hoa, South Vietnam. A room full of Vietnamese, including children, watched Armed Forces

Television, watched Batman, Matt Dillon, and other shows from a distant continent. Here was their glimpse of the world from which the Americans around them had come. I wanted to tell them that what they were watching on television represented *no place*, represented no neighborhoods from which the young Americans around them came. And I began to wonder, knowing that not even the makers of such shows lived in such worlds, whose real world does television represent?

There are traces of local authenticity and local variety on national television. *All in the Family* takes the cameras into a neighborhood in Queens. The accents, gestures, methods and perceptions of the leading actors in *Kojak* reflect in an interesting and accurate way the ethnic sensibilities of several neighborhoods in New York. The clipped speech of Jack Webb in *Dragnet* years ago was an earlier break from "televisionese." But, in general, television is an organ of nationalization, of homogenization—and, indeed, of a certain systematic inaccuracy about the actual, concrete texture of life in the United States.

This nationalizing effect also spills over into the news and the documentaries. The cultural factors which deeply affect the values and perceptions of various American communities are neglected; hence the treatment of problems affecting such communities is frequently oversimplified. This is especially true when matters of group conflict are involved. The tendency of newsmen is subtly to take sides and to regard some claims or behavior as due to "prejudice," others as rather more moral and commendable.

The mythic forms and story lines of the news and documentaries are not inconsonant with the mythic forms represented in the adventure stories and Westerns. "Good" and "evil" are rather clearly placed in conflict. "Hard-hitting" investigative reporting is mythically linked to classic American forms of moral heroism: the crimebuster, the incorruptible sheriff. The forces of law and progress ceaselessly cut into the jungle of corruption. There is continuity between the prime-time news and prime-time programming—much more continuity than is detected by the many cultivated Cyclopses who disdain "the wasteland" and praise the documentaries. The mythic structure of both is harmonious.

It should prove possible to mark out the habits of perception and mind encouraged by national television. If these categories are not decisive, better ones can surely be discerned. We might then design ways of instructing ourselves and our children in countervailing habits. It does not seem likely that the mind and heart tutored by many years of watching television (in doses of five or six hours a day) is in the same circumstance as the mind and heart never exposed to television. Education and criticism must, it seems, take this difference into account.

2. The Class Bias of Television

Television has had two striking effects. On the one hand, as Norman Podhoretz has remarked, it has not seemed to prevent people from reading; more books are being published and mass marketed than ever before in American history. It is possible that television stimulates many to go beyond what television itself can offer.

Secondly, television works, or appears to work, as a homogenizing medium. It presents a fairly non-representative, non-concrete, imagined world to a national audience. In many respects, it could be shown, the overall ideological tendency of television productions—from the news, through the talk shows, to the comedy hours, variety shows, and adventure, crime, and family shows—is that of a vague and misty liberalism: belief in the efficacy of an ultimate optimism, "talking through one's problems," a questioning of institutional authorities, a triumph of good over evil. Even a show like *All in the Family,* beneath its bluster and its violation of verbal taboos, illustrates the unfailing victory of liberal points of view: Archie Bunker always loses. A truly mean and aggressive reactionary point of view is virtually non-existent. There is no equivalent on national television to *Human Events* and other right-wing publications, or to the network of right-wing radio shows around the nation. While many critics of right and left find prime-time television to be a "wasteland," few have accused it of being fascist, malicious, evil, or destructive of virtue, progress, and hope. Television's liberalism is calculated to please neither the new radicals nor the classic liberals of the left, nor the upbeat, salesmanlike exponents of the right. In harmony with the images of progress built into both liberalism and capitalism, television seems, however gently, to undercut traditional institutions and to promote a restless, questioning attitude. The main product—and attitude—it has to sell is the new.

This attachment to the new insures that television will be a vaguely leftist medium, no matter who its personnel might be. Insofar as it debunks traditions and institutions—and even the act of *representing* these in selective symbolic form is a kind of veiled threat to them—television serves the purposes of that larger movement within which left and right (in America, at least) are rather like the two legs of locomotion: the movement of modernization. It serves, in general, the two mammoth institutions of modern life: the state and the great corporations. It serves these institutions even when it exalts the individual at the expense of family, neighborhood, religious organizations, and cultural groups. These are the only intermediate institutions that stand between the isolated individual and the massive institutions.

Thus the homogenizing tendencies of television are ambivalent. Television can electrify and unite the whole nation, creating an instantaneous network in which millions are simultaneous recipients of the same powerful images. But to what purpose, for whose use, and to what effect? Is it an unqualified good that the national grid should become so pre-eminent, superior to any and all local checks and balances? The relative national power and influence of state governors seems to have been weakened, for example; a state's two senators, by comparison, occupy a national stage and can more easily become national figures.

But in at least five other ways national television projects a sense of reality that is not identical to the sense of reality actual individuals in their concrete environments share. Taken together, these five ways construct a national social reality that is not free of a certain class and even ethnic bias.

(1) The television set becomes a new instrument of reality—of "what's happening" in the larger, national world, of "where it's at." In some sense what isn't on television isn't quite real, is not part of the nationally shared world, will be nonexistent for millions of citizens. Three examples may suggest the power of this new sense of reality.

Experiments suggest (so I am told) that audiences confronted with simultaneous projection on a large movie screen and on a television set regularly and overwhelmingly end up preferring the image on the smaller set. The attraction of reality is somehow there.

On a political campaign, or at a sports event, individuals seem to seek to be on camera with celebrities, as if seeking to share in a precious and significant verification of their existence. A young boy in Pittsburgh exults, "I'm real!" as he interposes himself between the grinding cameras and a presidential candidate in the crowd. Not to be on television is to lack weight in national consciousness. Audience "participation" (the ancient platonic word for being) fills a great psychic hunger: to be human in the world that really counts.

Finally, anyone who has participated in a large-scale event comes to recognize vividly how strait and narrow is the gate between what has actually happened and what gets on television. For the millions who see the television story, of course, the story is the reality. For those who lived through a strenuous sixteen-hour day on the campaign trail, for example, it is always something of a surprise to see what "made" the television screen—or, more accurately, what the television screen made real. That artificial reality turns out to have far more substance for the world at large than the lived sixteen hours. According to the ancient *maya*, the world of flesh and blood is an illusion. And so it is.

(2) Television is a new technology and depends upon sophisticated crafts. It is a world of high profit. Its inside world is populated by persons in a high income bracket. Moreover, television is a world that requires a great deal of travel, expense-account living, a virtual shuttle service between Los Angeles and New York, a taste for excellent service and high prestige. These economic factors seriously color television's image of the world.

The glitter of show business quickly spread to television. In the blossomy days when thinkers dreamed of an affluent society and praised the throwaway society, the shifting and glittering sets of television make-believe seemed like a metaphor for modern society. Actually, a visit to a television studio is extraordinarily disappointing, far more so, even, than a visit to an empty circus tent after the crowd has gone. Cheaply painted pastel panels, fingerprints sometimes visible upon them, are wheeled away and stacked. The cozy intimacy one shares from one's set at home is rendered false by the cavernous lofts of the studio, the tangle of wires, the old clothing and cynical buzzing of the bored technicians, crews, and hangers-on. Dust and empty plastic coffee cups are visible in corners where chairs compete for space. There is a tawdriness behind the scenes.

In a word, the world of television is a radically duplicitous world. Its illusions pervade every aspect of the industry. The salaries paid to those who greet the public remove them from the public. The settings in which they work are those of show business. Slick illusion is the constant temptation and establishes the rules of the game.

Moreover, the selling of products requires images of upward mobility. The sets, designs, and fluid metaphors of the shows themselves must suggest a certain richness, smoothness, and adequacy. It is not only that writers and producers understand that what audiences desire is escape. (One can imagine a poor society in which television would focus on limited aspiration and the dramas of reality.) It is also the case, apparently, that an inner imperative drives writers, producers, and sponsors to project their *own* fantasies. Not all Americans, by far, pursue upward mobility as a way of life. A great many teach their children to have modest expectations and turn down opportunities for advancement and mobility that would take them away from their familiar worlds.

The myths of the upwardly mobile and the tastes of the very affluent govern the visual symbols, the flow, and the chatter of television.

(3) The class bias of television reality proceeds not only from the relative economic affluence of the industry and its personnel. It springs as well from the educational level. "Televisionese" sends a clear and distinct message to the people, a message of exclusion and superiority. (George Wallace sends the message *back*; he is not its originator, only its echo.) It is common for a great many of the personnel connected with television to imagine themselves as anti-establishment and also perhaps as iconoclastic. Surely they must know that to men who work in breweries or sheet metal plants, to women who clean tables in cafeterias or splice wires in electronic assembly plants, they must seem to be at the very height of the Establishment. Their criticisms of American society—reflected in *Laugh-In*, in the night-club entertainers, and even in the dialogue of virtually every crime or adventure show—are perceived to be something like the complaints of spoiled children. There seems to be a self-hatred in the medium, a certain shame about American society, of which Lawrence Welk's old-fashioned, honeyed complacency and the militant right-

eousness of Bob Hope, John Wayne, and *Up With America!* are the confirming opposites. To confuse the hucksterism of television with the real America is, of course, a grievous error.

Television is a parade of experts instructing the unenlightened about the weather, aspirins, toothpastes, the latest books or proposals for social reform, and the correct attitudes to have with respect to race, poverty, social conflict, and new moralities. Television is preeminently a world of intellectuals. Academic persons may be astonished to learn of it and serious writers and artists may hear the theme with withering scorn, but for most people in the United States television is the medium through which they meet an almost solid phalanx of college-educated persons, professionals, experts, thinkers, authorities, and "with it," "swinging" celebrities: i.e., people unlike themselves who are drawn from the top ten percent of the nation in terms of educational attainment.

It is fashionable for intellectuals to disdain the world of television (although some, when asked, are known to agree to appear on it without hesitation). Yet when they appear on television they do not seem to be notably superior to the announcers, interviewers, and performers who precede them on camera or share the camera with them. (Incidentally, although many sports journalists write or speak condescendingly of "the jocks," when athletes appear as television announcers—Joe Garagiola, Sandy Koufax, Frank Gifford, Alex Karras, and others—the athletes seem not one whit inferior in intelligence or in sensitivity to the journalists.) Television is the greatest instrument the educated class has ever had to parade its wares before the people. On television that class has no rival. Fewer than ten percent of the American population has completed four years of college. That ten percent totally dominates television.

It is important to understand that the disdain for "popular culture" often heard in intellectual circles is seriously misplaced. Television, at least, more nearly represents the world of the educated ten percent than it reflects the world of the other ninety percent. At most, one might say in defense, the world of television represents the educated class's fantasies about the fantasies of the population. To say that *kitsch* has always required technicians to create it is not a sufficient route of escape. Do really serious intellectuals (i.e., not those "mere" technicians) have better understandings of where the people truly are? What, then, are those better understandings?

The interviews recorded by Robert Coles, for example, tend to show that persons of the social class represented by Archie Bunker are at least as complicated, many-sided, aware of moral ambiguities, troubled and sensitive, as the intellectuals who appear on television, in novels, or in the cinema. Artists who might use the materials of ordinary life for their creations are systematically separated from ordinary people by the economic conditions of creativity in the United States.

(4) The writers, producers, actors, and journalists of television are separated from most of the American population not only by economic

standing, and not only by education, but also by the culture in which their actual lives are lived out. By "culture" I mean those implicit, lived criteria that suggest to each of us what is real, relevant, significant, meaningful in the buzzing confusion of our experience: how we select out and give shape to our world. The culture of prime-time television is, it appears, a serious dissolvant of the cultures of other Americans. The culture of television celebrates to an extraordinary degree two mythic strains in the American character: the lawless and the irreverent. On the first count, stories of cowboys, gangsters, and spies still preoccupy the American imagination. On the second, the myth of "enlightenment" from local standards and prejudices still dominates our images of self-liberation and sophistication. No doubt the stronghold of a kind of priggish righteousness in several layers of American history leads those who rebel to find their rebellion all too easy. It is as though the educated admonish one another that they "can't go home again" and that the culture against which they rebel is solid and unyielding.

But what if it isn't? What if the perception of culture on the part of millions is, rather, that chaos and the jungle are constantly encroaching and that the rule of good order is threatened in a dozen transactions every day—by products that don't work, by experts and officials who take advantage of lay ignorance, by muggings and robberies, by jobs and pensions that disappear, by schools that do not work in concert with the moral vision of the home?

Television keeps pressing on the barriers of cultural resistance to obscenities, to some forms of sexual behavior, and to various social understandings concerning work and neighborhood and family relationships. A reporter from the *New York Times* reports with scarcely veiled satisfaction that *Deep Throat* is being shown in a former church in a Pennsylvania mining town, as though this were a measure of spreading enlightenment. It might be. But what if our understanding of how cultural, social, and moral strands are actually interwoven in the consciousness of peoples is inadequate? What if the collapse of moral inhibition in one area, for a significant number of persons, encourages a collapse at other places? What if moral values cannot be too quickly changed without great destructiveness? The celebration of "new moralities" may not lead to the kind of "humanization" cultural optimists anticipate.

Television, and the mass media generally, have vested interests in new moralities. The excitement of transgressing inhibitions is gripping entertainment. There are, however, few vested interests wishing to strengthen the inhibitions which make such transgressions good entertainment. Television is only twenty-five years old. We have very little experience or understanding proportionate to the enormous moral stakes involved. It is folly to believe that *laissez-faire* works better in moral matters than in economic matters or that enormous decisions in these matters are not already being made in the absence of democratic consent. When one kind of show goes on the air others are excluded during that time. The present system is effectively a form of social control.

I do not advocate any particular solution to this far-ranging moral dilemma; I do not know what to recommend. But the issue is a novel one for a free society, and we do not even have a well-thought-out body of options from which to choose. In that vacuum a rather-too-narrow social class is making the decisions. The pressures of the free market (so they say) now guide them. Is that so? Should it be so?

(5) Because of the structure and history of the social class that produces prime-time television, group conflict in the United States is also portrayed in a simplistic and biased way. The real diversity of American cultures and regions is shrouded in public ignorance. Occasional disruptions, like the rebellion of West Virginia miners against certain textbooks and the rebellion of parents in South Boston against what they perceived as downward mobility for their children and themselves, are as quickly as possible brushed from consciousness. America is pictured as though it were divided between one vast homogeneous "middle America," to be enlightened, and the enlighteners. In fact, there are several "middle Americas."

There is more than one important Protestant culture in our midst. The Puritan inheritance is commonly exaggerated and the evangelical, fundamentalist inheritance is vastly underestimated (and under-studied). Hubert Humphrey is from a cultural stream different from that of George Wallace or of John Lindsay. There are also several quite significant cultural streams among Catholics; the Irish of the Middle West (Eugene McCarthy, Michael Harrington) often have a quite different cultural tradition from the Irish of Philadelphia, Boston, or New York. Construction workers on Long Island are not offended by "pornography" in the same way as druggists in small midwestern towns; look inside their cabs and helmets, listen to their conversations, if you seek evidence. There is also more than one cultural stream among American Jews; the influence of the Jews of New York has probably misled us in our understanding of the Jewish experience in America.

It seems, moreover, that the social class guiding the destiny of television idealizes certain ethnic groups—the legitimate minorities—even while this class offers in its practices no greater evidence of genuine egalitarianism than other social classes. At the same time this class seems extremely slow to comprehend the experiences of other American cultures. One of the great traumas of human history was the massive migration to America during the last 100 years. It ought to be one of the great themes of high culture, and popular culture as well. Our dramatists neglect it.

Group conflict has, moreover, been the rule in every aspect of American life, from labor to corporate offices to neighborhoods to inter-ethnic marriages. Here, too, the drama is perhaps too real and vivid to be touched: *these* are inhibitions the liberal culture of television truly respects. Three years ago one could write that white ethnics, like some others, virtually never saw themselves on television; suddenly we have had *Banacek, Colombo, Petrocelli,*

Kojak, Kolchack, Rhoda, Sanford, and *Chico.* Artists are still exploring the edges of how much reality can be given voice and how to voice it. These are difficult, even explosive matters. Integrity and care are required.

It must seem odd to writers and producers to be accused of having a "liberal" bias when they are so aware of the limitations they daily face and the grueling battles they daily undergo. But why do they have these battles except that they have a point of view and a moral passion? We are lucky that the social class responsible for the creative side of television is not a reactionary and frankly illiberal class. Still, that it is a special class is itself a problem for all of us, including those involved in it.

Footnotes

1. *There is no discernible variation between the hours spent watching television by the college-educated, or by professors and journalists, and the public as a whole.*

2. *The second theme is explored in more detail in my essay, "The People and the News," appearing in* Moments of Truth? *(The Fifth Alfred I. duPont-Columbia University Survey of Broadcast Journalism), Marvin Barrett, ed. New York: Thomas Y. Crowell Company, 1975.*

Those of us who have been around quite a while imagine that we learn through speech and through the word. Perhaps we do. But there is no evidence that young children learn that way. All the evidence is that they learn by observation and imitation. . . . Television is a medium of gestural communication. It's a medium of auditory communication, of emotional feelings as well as speech content. And it is a medium which reaches the illiterate or the non-literate, including young children. Moreover, the medium is present in the child's ecological niche, the home. This makes it almost unique. . . . These are the reasons why social scientists are fascinated by the effects of television upon children and can scarcely believe that the effects are not important.

Alberta Siegel

Understanding Television: An Overview of the Literature of the Medium as a Social and Cultural Force

Richard Adler

The introduction of television in this country coincided with the beginning of a remarkable, unprecedented period of change in American society. In many ways television seems a particularly appropriate symbol for the combination of affluence and upheaval, of complacency and confusion which marked the post-war era. There is no question but that television has reflected many of the social and cultural changes of the past twenty-five years. A more interesting, though more difficult question is the degree to which television has contributed to the shaping of these events. In other words, what role has television itself played in the development of contemporary American society?

As Stephen Graubard has pointed out, the invention of movable-type printing in the fifteenth century created the conditions that permitted not only the spread of mass literacy but made possible—perhaps even inevitable—the Reformation and the scientific revolution which transformed the societies of the West. Since the introduction of television has been equated in importance with the advent of printing, it is fair to ask whether any similar, though almost certainly less monumental effects can be attributed to the rise of television.

Like printing, television clearly represents a fundamental change in the way people communicate with each other over distance. But in trying to understand the meaning of this change the most obvious difficulty is our lack of perspective on this new medium. We can now interpret the significance of printing from the vantage point of more than five centuries; television has existed for barely a generation. Within this brief time span, however, a system has been created which reaches into virtually every home and is encountered daily by virtually every citizen of the country. The pace of the development of

Richard Adler is Assistant Director of the Aspen Institute Program on Communications and Society and Coordinator of its Workshop on Television.

television is a striking example of the "acceleration of history" which marks the twentieth century.

The purpose of this essay is to review some of the major attempts to interpret television's impact as a social and cultural force. I have been able to be neither wholly comprehensive nor thoroughly systematic in my selections. But I have tried to provide a rough topography of the principal approaches to understanding television's role in American society, beginning with pioneering predictions about the medium, proceeding through continuing efforts to assess its effects, and ending with recent applications of sophisticated social science methodologies to describe how television functions. Several related areas of the literature of television, though valuable, have had to be excluded because of the limitations of space. These include technical works on the technology of the medium, on legal issues, and on techniques of production; the thousands of individual empirical studies of viewer behavior and response (though several works which synthesize this research are included); and works on television in countries other than the United States.

Even with these exclusions the remaining body of literature is large and diverse and resists easy summary. The phenomenon of television has been approached from a variety of points of view—economic, sociological, psychological, political, esthetic—which often seem to have little to do with one another. And while there is general agreement that television has become the most dominant of the media, there is little consensus in the literature as to what this means. One of the principal conclusions of this review is that there is a large and still widening gap between what has been asserted about the effect of television and what has been established and generally accepted as fact.

As I have suggested, the very success of television may be responsible for this uncertainty. Television grew so rapidly that there has hardly been time to examine its significance. Moreover, the demographic growth of television was matched by technological changes which altered and extended the nature of the medium: the size of sets shrank even as screens grew larger; instantaneous national distribution was made possible by coast-to-coast coaxial cable; crude kinescope recordings gave way to videotape which was virtually indistinguishable from live programming; color was introduced; solid state technology made sets—and cameras—lighter and more portable; instant replay was perfected; communications satellites abolished the barrier of distance by enabling direct transmission from any point on the globe. By the time Neil Armstrong set foot on the moon, it seemed only natural that the event should be carried around the world on live color television.

Trying to gauge the impact of television on American society in the past twenty-five years has been something like attempting to understand the dynamics of a tidal wave—when one is in the middle of it. In his history of modern America, Daniel Boorstin characterizes the effect of the arrival of television as not merely a "revolution" but a "cataclysm."[1] Only the automobile, he believes, has done more to transform the quality of everyday life in America.

Among other things, television has become the primary form of entertainment and the most relied-on source of news for most Americans/It has created new relationships between the populace and their leaders and the events of the day. It has altered our notions of time and space, abolishing distances and helping to accelerate the pace of history. It is a major force in the acculturation of children, probably next in importance only to parental influence. It has become a fundamental component of the corporate marketing structure which underlies our consumer economy. In short, television has become part of the total environment in which we live.

Yet even today almost no one takes television seriously. It has become merely another piece of furniture in the home, looked to for the most part to provide undemanding diversion. Its usual blandness and banality, its repetitiveness, its endless commercial intrusions are accepted as inevitable. Outside of a few special-interest groups, the agencies directly concerned with its regulation, and a small body of communications researchers, issues of the nature and content of our television system have been accorded low priority in the national consciousness.

Paradoxically, it may be that the reason television is not taken seriously is precisely because it is so important. It has become so inextricably woven into the social fabric that it is extremely difficult to view it as an institution in its own right. Much more than a form of entertainment, television has become the principal means by which Americans maintain contact with the daily flow of national life.

Defining Television

A final difficulty in attempting to determine television's role in society is that it is not a simple phenomenon. The word itself encompasses at least three separate, though related aspects of a complex system. All three are necessary and interdependent, but each makes a distinctive contribution to making "television" what it is. These three components are worth noting before turning to the literature of the medium:

(1) The television *set*—the device which inhabits the living room or bedroom or den of more than 97 percent of all American households; which displays a smallish electronic image of fairly poor resolution and emits sounds of even poorer fidelity; and which succeeds in capturing an astonishing amount of the attention of the American people. One explanation that has been offered for its peculiar fascination is that the television set has replaced the old family hearth—it glows, emits sounds, and provides a focal point around which the family can orient itself. (The pattern of television as a single focal point,

however, does seem to be changing as more families acquire multiple sets: more than 40 percent of American households now contain two or more sets.)

There is considerable evidence of the value Americans place on access to television. The total value of sets in this country represents an investment of more than $10 billion by individuals and families. Moreover, data from the cable television industry indicates that more than 7½ million American households willingly pay $5-6 per month for improved television reception. In areas in which off-the-air reception is poor or nonexistent, 80 or 90 percent or more of the homes accessible to cable service will subscribe. Perhaps the most suggestive evidence comes from recent experiments conducted in Germany and England in which groups of families were paid *not* to watch television. In both cases, all participants dropped out of the experiment within a few months (well short of the expected duration) and had turned their sets back on. For these families, at least, television seems to have become a necessity.

(2) The television *production/distribution* system. The set is, of course, not a self-contained device like a toaster or music box. It is a receiver, the end-point of a gigantic distribution system capable of transmitting signals instantaneously from a single point to those millions of sets in all those homes across the country. In the early days of television, a decision was made by the Federal Communications Commission to foster a policy of "localism"—that is, to license many relatively low-power stations throughout the country, with the number of stations in each community generally correlated to population. In actual fact, however, the industry quickly came to be dominated by the three national networks whose programs are now available, either by direct broadcast or by cable, almost everywhere in the country.

An important consequence of this network-dominated system is that American television is highly *national* in character. Ninety percent of all television hours watched are broadcast by the three national networks. Popular network programs are seen by a substantial portion of the American population, and events like the Super Bowl, the Academy Awards, the quadrennial political conventions, even the showing of certain "blockbuster" movies, take on the character of national rituals because of the electronic participation of such a large percentage of the population. A schematic diagram of the American television system would show signals *flowing one way* from a relatively few sources to a very large number of recipients.

A second consequence of this massive distribution system is that television is a highly attractive medium for national advertising. No magazine reaches as many people as a popular network program. Television has helped create new kinds of mass national markets, and the use of television advertising has become almost obligatory for any company which wishes to inject its product into the national consciousness.

When the phrase "the power of television" is used it usually refers to the medium's capacity for instantaneous diffusion of its messages to a huge aggregate audience. That this capacity makes television both a vital national communications link *and* an unparalleled vehicle for commercial advertising has been a subject of increasing concern. This issue is discussed more fully below, in the section on Television as a Business.

(3) The *content* of television. Most of the literature on television to date has been concerned with the implications of the two aspects of the medium just discussed. The area in which the meaning of television should be most apparent—the nature and quality of its content—has received least consideration. Most regular viewers, according to available evidence, are generally content with the programming offered to them; most critics and intellectuals find it easy to agree with Newton Minow's characterization of television as a "vast wasteland." Between these two poles is largely a vacuum.

Reasons for the lack of serious attention to the content of television are not difficult to find: a ratings-dominated system *does* produce programs which are banal, trivial, stereotyped, and repetitious, intended to keep as many people as possible watching until the next commercial break. And there is so much of it: each year produces thousands of episodes of hundreds of programs, turned out assembly-line fashion to satisfy the medium's voracious appetite for material. In addition, the small size of the television screen and the domestic setting in which it is viewed seem to militate against the intense concentration required by complexity of thought or plot. As a result, television almost always presents simplified versions of reality.

Yet none of these constraints mean that the medium is devoid of content that can and does generate genuine emotional involvement and communicate ideas and attitudes to vast audiences. At a minimum, its programs represent a rich repository of images and values shared daily by a majority of Americans. Beyond this lies the question of how these messages shape Americans' perceptions of their society and of themselves. What the literature has to say about these questions is the subject of this paper.

Early Studies (1935-1960)

The ability to broadcast moving images and sound was achieved in the late 1920's, but World War II postponed the full-scale commercial introduction of television until the late 1940's. One of the earliest essays about television, written well before its arrival in the home, has proved to be one of the most prescient. Rudolf Arnheim's "A Forecast of Television" was published in 1935 in *Intercine,* the journal of the International Institute for Educational Film.[2] While Arnheim acknowledges that the ability to send pictures and sounds over great distances still seemed "uncanny," he explained that this new invention was merely an application of well-known laws of light, sound, electrical propagation, and human vision and hearing. Arnheim also realized that television seemed "magical and mysterious" because it was unfamiliar; he felt that once "television sets have appeared on the birthday tables and under the Christmas trees" their novelty would fade and curiosity about the medium would disappear. So he proposed to "take advantage of the propitious moment" to speculate about what television would likely come to mean.

Arnheim viewed television as the logical development of man's desire to extend his perceptions beyond the reach of his unaided senses. But adding sight to sound would create a medium radically different from radio. Hearing, Arnheim argued, "excels in transmitting speech and music, that is, the products of the spirit; it renders little of physical reality ... the ear is the tool of reasoning, it is best qualified to receive material that has already been given shape by man." Television will add a wholly new dimension, he felt, since "seeing is direct experience, the gathering of sensory raw material."

Arnheim welcomed the "concreteness of experience" which television would convey, but he warned that it might encourage the development of "a cult of sensory stimulation," substituting direct experience for the more demanding task of understanding:

> *Television is a new, hard test of our wisdom. If we succeed in mastering the new medium it will enrich us. But it can also put our mind to sleep. We must not forget that in the past the inability to transport immediate experience and to convey it to others made the use of language necessary and thus compelled the human mind to develop concepts. For in order to describe things one must draw the general from the specific; one must select, compare, think. When communication can be achieved by pointing with the finger, however, the mouth grows silent, the writing hand stops, and the mind shrinks.*

Arnheim concludes by speculating that the experiences provided by television may prove so beguiling that they may come to be accepted as a substitute for life itself. While this dark prophecy has failed to fully materialize, it describes a phenomenon which later commentators have observed and captures a feeling which a sensitive television viewer will recognize:

> *Television will make up for actual physical presence even more complete than does radio. All the more isolated will be the individual in his retreat, and the balance of trade will be correspondingly precarious: an enormous influx of riches, consumption without services in return. The pathetic hermit, squatting in his room, hundreds of miles away from the scene that he experiences as his present life, the "viewer" who cannot even laugh or applaud without feeling ridiculous, is the final product of a century-long development, which has*

*led from the campfire, the market place, and arena to the lonesome
consumer of spectacles today.*

The first full-length book about television, published four years
before Arnheim's essay, also attempts to foresee the future of the medium,
although its speculations are much more practical than Arnheim's. As its title
implies, *Television: Its Methods and Uses* by Edgar Felix is concerned with both
technology and applications.[3] In one of these areas, as it turns out, Felix was
extremely short-sighted; in the other he proves to be devastatingly accurate.

When the book appeared in 1931, the developers of television had
achieved the ability to transmit a crude 60-line image which could yield a barely
discernible image of a human face. Both camera and set utilized mechanical
spinning discs to break down the image into scanning lines. It was clear that this
was not a satisfactory solution and that a commercially acceptable system would
require a considerably improved picture. Felix was confident that research then
under way would soon perfect a system capable of transmitting a picture of 100
or even 200 lines, but he expressed grave doubts that a picture containing more
lines (and hence, greater detail) would be attainable, because of the massive
band-width required. At best, he felt, a 200-line image could provide sufficient
detail to present a scene containing two persons; coverage of sports events and
telecasting movies would be impossible. Of course, Felix was completely wrong
about attainable image quality; current American television contains a 525-line
image, while systems in Europe and elsewhere utilize more than 600 lines. While
Felix mentioned the cathode ray tube—the key to all modern television—he cited
it only in passing as one of a number of possible devices under investigation at
the time.

In retrospect, Felix's technological descriptions and speculations
seem quaint, even humorous. In another area, however—the economics of the
future television system—he was a much better prophet. While Felix recognized a
great deal of uncertainty about the technology of the medium, he saw almost
none about how it would be supported: "The prospects that television will be
supported by means other than advertising appear exceedingly remote." He
realized, correctly, that the battle over this issue had already been fought and
won (or lost, depending on one's perspective):

> *The precedents established by sound broadcasting apply so logical-
> ly to television that it will be next to impossible to establish the
> newer field on a different basis . . . Television will find a complete
> structure ready to commercialize it. Broadcasting stations have
> organized personnel and established contacts in the advertising field,
> the advertising agencies have specialists in handling radio problems
> for their clients, and the advertiser is already accustomed to radio as
> a medium of approach to the public. Advertising will be ready for*

the visual medium long before the medium is ready for advertising. *[Emphasis added.]*

When Felix describes exactly how advertisers will use television, he does so in terms that sound not in the least dated: "The cigar advertiser who appeals to the young man can actually demonstrate that cigar smoking will make any young man look like a major executive . . . a reproduction of a luscious strawberry shortcake is much more effective in creating an appetite than any word-of-mouth description . . ." Felix's *Television* suggests that whatever confusion there has been (and continues to be) about the nature and effects of television, it was clear from the beginning that it would become, in this country at least, what Felix called "the most powerful medium for sales stimulation."

Although the full-scale arrival of television took longer than either Arnheim or Felix expected, both underestimated the attraction of its novelty once it became available. While less than one out of a hundred American homes had a television set in 1947, 25 percent had acquired one by 1951. Just two years later, sets were in half of all households. By 1956, barely a decade after its introduction, more than 75 percent of the population had invested a total of $10 billion to purchase sets. By the end of the 1960's, television ownership in America had become virtually universal.

The somber note about television's impact struck by Arnheim never completely faded out of the literature. During the late 1940's and early 1950's skeptical articles appeared periodically with titles like "How Illiterate Can Television Make Us?", "Television: Boon or Bane?", "TV: A Mixed Blessing," and, more ominously, "Hypnosis in the Living Room" and "Video Slavery."[4]

Despite this negative strain, early investigations by social scientists portrayed television as a generally benign force. One of the most obvious effects of television was that it was rapidly displacing other leisure-time activities such as radio-listening, movie-going, and reading. A study by two sociologists at Rutgers University, sponsored by CBS and published in 1949, indicated that this displacement effect was already "significant."[5] Among the study's other findings were that television was adding a "completely new dimension" to the experience of children; and was "stimulating new interests within the family," a new "awareness of family unity," and "was enlarging the immmediate circle of social relationships."

Subsequent research during the following decade was not quite so glowingly positive, but the general thrust of the studies was that television was relatively innocuous. In 1956 Leo Bogart published his massive attempt to compile all available studies into a composite portrait of *The Age of Television.*[6] His book is lucidly written and remains a useful source of data on the early years of television. (A new edition, issued in 1972, contains a large selection of additional notes which update the 1956 findings.) The book is filled with tables which summarize such things as "Growth of Homes Owning Radio and Television," "A Comparison of Women in TV and Non-TV Households," "TV Viewing in Big Cities and Small Towns," "TV's Effect on Radio Listening," "Purchases Before and After Owning a TV Set," and "Daily Time Spent Watching Television, by School Grade." Most of the information in the book was derived from questionnaire-type studies in which viewers were asked to report on their attitudes toward television and its effects on their lives.

One of the book's most impressive findings concerned the degree to which television had displaced other leisure-time activities. Bogart stated that by 1956 "television had achieved indisputable ascendancy over the other mass media." When 2,000 New York residents were asked "If you could have only one of these four, which would you prefer?", 50 percent chose television, 32 percent newspapers, 15 percent radio and 3 percent magazines. He then went on to detail the drastic impact of television on radio listening time and movie attendance. Bogart also concluded that reading had been affected: "There is overwhelming agreement that television has reduced the amount of time which the American people spend reading magazines and books, [but] not newspapers. The effects appear to be substantial, even though they may be somewhat lessened as television becomes a long-established feature of family life."

When he turned to measuring the broader social consequences of television, Bogart's conclusions were much less clear-cut. He does suggest that the Rutgers finding that television "enlarges the immediate circle of social relationships" was a temporary phenomenon which existed only as long as television sets were owned by a minority of the population. As soon as most people had acquired sets, they began to stay home and watch by themselves. Bogart reported that by 1956, adult television watchers tended to be less active in social organizations and to go out less in the evening. They also tended to purchase name-brand products more frequently than non-viewers. But he offered little evidence of more significant changes in basic attitudes, life styles, or behavior.

Perhaps the most revealing chapter in the book concerns "Television and the Juvenile Audience," a subject which was to become a center of increasing controversy. By 1956 the average school child in grades 1-8 was watching television over three hours per day. Bogart cites studies which indicated that television has disrupted the eating and sleeping schedules of some children and led to conflicts between parents and children over program choices. But he also reported that a majority of parents believe that television has been "good for their children." In almost every case in which television has been charged with substantial effects, Bogart suspended judgement. The following is typical:

> *There would seem to be some potential dangers in the common prac-*
> *tice of using TV as a baby sitter, if the net effect is to reduce the*

amount of direct attention the child receives from his parents, or the extent to which he participates in family life. However, it is difficult to trace any damage done to the child's emotional well-being in this respect, for if TV is interposed between children and parents this usually reflects attitudes and behavior expressed by the parents in other ways as well.

On the subject of the possible harmful effects of televised violence, Bogart quoted at length the views of authorities on both sides of the question. Although acknowledging the importance of the issue, Bogart concluded that the controversy has produced "more opinion than evidence"—and once again he suspended judgment.

The ambiguity of *The Age of Television* illustrates a problem which has characterized the discussion of television and its effects from its inception. Intelligent observers have expressed with absolute conviction their belief that television has wrought major changes among individuals, within their communities, and upon the very fabric of society. Yet the evidence produced by social science research tends to be either bland or inconclusive. To a large degree, it seems as if the critics and the researchers have operated in separate spheres, with scant communication between them.

Four years after *The Age of Television* was published another work appeared which lent further support to the notion that "hard research" indicated that television was unlikely to produce significant social changes. Like Bogart's book, Joseph T. Klapper's *The Social Effects of Mass Communications* was a synthesis of existing research.[7] Klapper's work dealt only in part with television, but it has affected much of the subsequent debate about the medium. The major conclusion of the book was simple and clear:

Persuasive mass communication functions far more frequently as an agent of reinforcement than as an agent of change. Conversion is typically found to be the most rare. The efficacy of mass communication in influencing existing opinion and attitude is inversely correlated with the degree of change.

Thus, according to Klapper, television (as a form of mass communications) was more likely to be a conservative than a revolutionary force. Still, Klapper by no means concluded that mass media were wholly without effect. On the question of the effects of media violence on young viewers, for example, he could not be very reassuring:

. . . although research has contributed greatly to our knowledge of the effects of media depictions of crime and violence, it has not

faced the socially important question of whether such material is in an overall sense socially harmful or socially innocuous . . . We may hope that those for whom violence is not innocuous comprise only a minority of the nation's children. But we do not know that they are a minority and in any case the absolute number is not likely to be insignificant. Our present and very limited knowledge suggests that the group may include an unstable portion of those children who are peer-group oriented, of those children who for one reason or another are often frustrated, and of those children who are maladjusted in various ways. The total number of such children cannot be small, and even if it were, any influence contributing to the continuance or intensification of their difficulties can hardly be dismissed as unimportant. If depictions of crime and violence have an unhealthy effect upon even one percent of the nation's children, it becomes socially important to inquire whether and how the situation can be rectified.

As we will see shortly, this issue—despite a good deal of research since 1960—remains very much unresolved.

Also, even if the media merely reinforced existing values, the question could be (and was) raised: just which values and attitudes were being reinforced by television?

Television as a Business

During the 1960's the novelty of television wore off, as Arnheim had predicted. But the spread of television continued unabated as color was introduced, as an increasing number of families became multiple set owners, and as the total number of hours watched crept steadily upward. By the end of the decade there would be over 800 stations on the air, broadcasting on UHF as well as VHF band. With the assistance of cable systems extending reception into remote areas, the saturation of America was virtually complete.

But something else happened in the 1960's: the earlier years of the medium began to be regarded as the Golden Age of Television. This was in part a matter of sheer nostalgia. But it also grew out of a sense that television had failed to live up to its promise of bringing the world at large to the home viewer. And the overall quality of programming seemed to decline; "Studio One," "Omnibus," "See It Now," and "Your Show of Shows" may not have been great art, but what followed them was worse, not better. A kind of predictable mediocrity had set in.

In *Television and Society*, published in 1956, Harry Skornia proposed that the way to understand television was not by asking viewers what they thought of it, nor by analyzing it as a medium of mass communications, by looking at television as an *industry*.[8]   Although in theory the air waves belonged to the public, the contents of television were in fact being determined on the basis of what would produce the largest revenues for the owners of the networks and stations. Television in this regard had simply followed the pattern of private ownership established by radio, but the problem was more acute for television because of the more limited number of available channels:

> *Perhaps never before in history have the most powerful channels to the people been so completely controlled by so small a segment of the national life . . . citizens have an image which is almost wholly dictated by sales-advertising-, and business-oriented custodians.*

Skornia's argument was quite simple: television in America is produced by profits. And since the revenues of television are solely based on advertising, and advertising dollars are directly related to the number of viewers reached by an advertisement, then program ratings become the single overwhelming criterion determining program choices. These constraints offer little room for excellence, experiment, or controversy.

Skornia's intention was not to try to instill a conscience in the controllers of commercial television but to point out that there is a basic incompatibility between "public or overall national interest [and] those practices which a business corporation, created to operate for a profit, *must* observe in a competitive environment."

This argument was restated and amplified in a series of books which followed, including Nicholas Johnson's *How To Talk Back To Your Television Set* (1970) and Les Brown's *Televi$ion: The Business Behind the Box* (1971).[9] Also in this category is Fred Friendly's *Due to Circumstances Beyond Our Control* (1967).[10] The latter book is unusual because it is the account of an insider: Friendly describes his experience with Edward R. Murrow in pioneering video journalism and his later career as President of CBS News. The book ends, however, with his resignation in protest over a decision to carry another rerun of *I Love Lucy* rather than a Congressional hearing on Vietnam. Friendly's well-publicized departure from CBS became a dramatic symbol of the victory of profits and ratings over the networks' sense of responsibility to the public.

Analysis of the implications of television as a business reached a new level of sophistication in 1973 with the publication of two important studies: *Economic Aspects of Broadcast Regulation* by Roger G. Noll, Merton J. Peck, and John J. McGowan, and Edward J. Epstein's *News from Nowhere*.[11] Both books provide important new information about how and why the American television system functions as it does.

Noll, Peck, and McGowan's major contribution is to demonstrate that our television has been shaped not merely by business practices but by the regulatory decisions made over the years by the Federal Communications Commission. Unlike Skornia and his fellow critics, they have no objections to a privately-owned television system run for profit, a system which they believe produces "enormous benefits" for the public. But they take strong issue with the F.C.C.'s policy of "localism," which they believe has not only failed to provide valued local service but has unnecessarily limited program choices which the audience desires and which could be supported by additional advertising revenues. The authors concede that their economic analyses do not yield much guidance about the social benefits or costs of particular kinds of programs. But they insist that their research does reveal a system which is economically inefficient and which provides its greatest benefits only to those fortunate enough to own commercial television licenses.

Edward J. Epstein's book focuses on one specific aspect of the television system—the national evening news programs of the three networks. Epstein's hypothesis is that every aspect of these programs—which stories are covered, which are broadcast, where they originate, how they are reported and by whom—is determined by the aims of the corporations which produce them. He carefully documents how the constraints of time, budget, audience, and federal regulation (requiring "balance and objectivity") dictate both form and content of national television news. Demolishing the news executives' claims that they are merely "holding a mirror up to reality," Epstein convincingly demonstrates that these programs provide a record of the day's events which is incomplete, superficial, and artificially melodramatic. In tracing the economic imperatives behind these limitations, Epstein also rejects the claim that national television news reflects the liberal bias of its reporters and producers. Personal beliefs, Epstein observes, are much weaker determinants than corporate policies.

News from Nowhere represents the most detailed examination of the consequences of a television system which is commercially sponsored, dependent on ratings, and operated for a profit. And although the book is confined to the analysis of only one kind of television program, it suggests that Epstein's approach and methodology (i.e., the study of the behavior of large organizations) could be fruitfully applied to other areas of television.

Television as a Medium

The publication of Marshall McLuhan's *Understanding Media* in 1964 injected a new viewpoint into the discussion of television's role in society. [12] The book was about much more than television; in fact, McLuhan insisted that a great number of surprising things, including the bicycle, clothing, and money, should be considered as media, a term he defined as "the extensions of man." But his comments on the electronic media and on television in particular attracted the most attention. The book has been much discussed, and there is no need to review it at length here.[13] But this overview would not be complete without an attempt to place this singular work in the context of the literature of television.

McLuhan's major contribution was to insist that television and the other electronic media are much more than interesting gadgets or convenient channels of entertainment and information; they are in effect new forces which are altering the very nature of man and his world. Television is making us all inhabitants of a universal "global village," just as the advent of the printing press was responsible (among other things) for the creation of industrialized nation-states. Relying on intuition and analogy rather than statistics or empirical evidence, McLuhan portrayed television as nothing less than a major landmark in the evolution of human consciousness.

These ideas attracted attention because they seemed to transcend more mundane concerns about such matters as the number of sets per household, the amount of television watching, or the impact a particular kind of program might have on its audience. McLuhan declared all such questions irrelevant. He particularly insisted that trying to understand television by examining the programs it offers is as futile as attempting to comprehend the impact of the printing press in the 15th century by interpreting the contents of Gutenberg's Bible.

Understanding Media succeeded in stirring up considerable interest in television among many who had come to take its presence for granted. Picking up a point Arnheim had made 30 years earlier (and later by Harold Innis), McLuhan argued that media are not neutral conveyors of messages: each medium appeals to and affects the balance of the senses in a different way. And because of television's ability to combine image and sound and transmit them instantaneously, television is the most powerful of the "extensions of man."

Unfortunately, however, McLuhan's book created as much confusion and misunderstanding as illumination. The opacity of his writing style made a thorough reading of *Understanding Media* an arduous task. The aphoristic nature of his assertions and his unwillingness to abide by traditional standards of scholarship forced his readers either to accept or reject his ideas *in toto*.

Either for these reasons or because of the unorthodoxy of its ideas, the ground broken by *Understanding Media* has yielded little subsequent fruit. McLuhan himself contributed to several lively popularizations of his ideas, but he has produced no major new writings over the past decade. Nor have others come forward to pick up the leads he offered. Like *Finnegans Wake,* a work greatly admired by McLuhan, *Understanding Media* seemed likely to take its place in the literature as an impressive but solitary landmark, a book more admired than read.

A recent book, however, does carry McLuhan's ideas forward in an interesting way. *The Responsive Chord* is not the work of a scholar but a practitioner.[14] Tony Schwartz began as a maker of recorded "sound documentaries" and later became a producer of radio and television commercials. His book is concerned with the use of sound in electronic media, principally for purposes of creating effective advertising. It is a mixture of practical advice and theorizing, and displays a kind of cheerful amorality characteristic of practical books about advertising. It also contains some important ideas about how television has created a new social environment.

Schwartz begins with the proposition that we fail to understand electronic media because traditional communications theory, on which we still rely, is inadequate "as a tool for analyzing the mass-media process." Schwartz concedes that the traditional theory, which he describes as based on a "transportation model" of communications, is useful for describing certain media, especially print. But, like McLuhan, he believes new theories are needed to understand new media.

Schwartz bases his own theory on the assumption that the basic conditions of communication have changed. Traditional theory envisions communication as an occasional activity requiring the expenditure of effort (to code, send, and decode a message). Today, Schwartz asserts, "a state of communication is nearly always present in our environment . . . Indeed one has to expend considerable effort hypothesizing a situation in our culture in which communication does not regularly occur." In this dynamic, information-laden environment the problem (particularly for an advertiser) is not how to get a message to a receiver but how to get his attention.

Within this competitive environment television is an especially potent medium, far more effective than print. It does not require an elaborate encoding and decoding of messages and brings into play a whole range of non-verbal forms of communication—intonation, gesture, expression, movement, color, etc. Schwartz suggests that our print-biased educations have desensitized us to these non-rational dimensions of communication, and he warns that we must learn to be aware of them if we are to cope successfully with the torrent of communications which surrounds us.

Schwartz is clearly a student of McLuhan, and he shares his mentor's faults as well as his virtues. His generalizations are sweeping, and his enthusiasm for the electronic revolution tempts him into overstatement. His arguments by analogy often seem strained. But his extensive practical experience makes much of the book convincing. The manipulative power Schwartz attributes to the skillful use of radio and television is disturbing. Even more disturbing is his contention that the standards we rely on to judge ethical communications have become outmoded. Though unlikely to become as celebrated as *Understanding Media*, *The Responsive Chord* should be required reading for anyone trying to understand television's role in society.

Television as a Social Force

Whether or not Schwartz is correct in considering traditional methods inadequate for understanding electronic media, it is undeniably true that a gap continues to widen between what has been asserted about the effects of television and what has been established or measured by social science research. Certainly the blame for this gap cannot be placed on the laxity of the social sciences. On the contrary, the past decade has been a period of unparalleled research activity in measuring the impact of television. In a few areas quite definitive results have been reached: It has been firmly established that virtually any subject that can be taught in a classroom can be effectively taught by means of television.[15] And research conducted on the impact of *Sesame Street* has demonstrated measurable gains in the cognitive skills of pre-school children.[16]

Social science research has been much less successful in identifying other effects of the medium, in particular harmful effects. The problems of social science in this area are clearly evident in the continuing effort to settle the disturbing issue of televised violence and children. This issue has been raised because television is one of the earliest social influences to enter a child's life: By the age of two and a half years, nearly a third of all children watch television regularly; by age six nearly all have become viewers. The impact of television on young children is of particular concern because their values and cognitive skills are still being developed. What is it our children are learning from television?

Much of the present state of knowledge on this question is contained in five large volumes of reports and papers commissioned by the Surgeon General's Scientific Advisory Committee on Television and Social Behavior and published in 1972.[17] The project had its origins in 1969, when Senator John Pastore wrote the Secretary of H.E.W. asking what appeared to be a simple question: is there "a causal connection between televised violence and crime and antisocial behavior by individuals, particularly children?" As a result of this inquiry the Surgeon General's Committee was set up to sponsor and evaluate a massive year-long program of research.

The results of this research appear in the five volumes. They contain not only studies focused directly on televised violence but also studies on a range of related subjects such as patterns of television use by children, the effects of televised advertising, television and social learning, and analyses of media content. Taken as a group they represent a rich variety of perspectives on the relationship between television and children. They also represent the most ambitious and costly single program of research on television's effects ever undertaken.

However, when the Surgeon General's Committee attempted to summarize the meaning of all this research—to answer Senatore Pastore's simple question—the answer was highly conditional:[18]

> *The evidence does indicate that televised violence may lead to increased aggressive behavior in certain subgroups of children, who might constitute a small portion or a substantial portion of young television viewers. We cannot estimate the size of the fraction, however . . . .*

It should be noted that several members of the Committee felt strongly that the accumulated evidence warranted a stronger conclusion. But the fact remains that the Committee was unable to reach a consensus on the issue. Their report admits that the evidence contains ambiguities and even contradictions—and that many more questions were raised by the research than were answered.[19]

One of the major lessons to be drawn from the Surgeon General's report is the limitation of studying the effects of television in terms of a particular televised action (or attitude) which is subsequently reproduced by someone who has viewed it. It would be convenient (though disturbing) if the impact of television were so simple. It now seems more likely that the effects of television take place indirectly and over time. They are also strongly conditioned by the environment of which television is but a part and by the past experiences and present disposition of the viewer.[20]

Having said this, I must also say that the accumulating evidence strongly suggests that television *does* have social consequences and that different contents have different effects. As research methodologies improve, progress will continue to be made in specifying the impact of television.[21] But this progress will be made slowly, and a generation of new questions will continue to outrace the finding of agreed-on answers.

A quite different approach to understanding television as a social force—one that has just begun to be explored—is provided by the perspective of the historian. The historian would seem especially well qualified to place the institution of television in a larger context and to examine its effects on other institutions. Yet very little such work has been done. One reason for this, suggested by Erik Barnouw, is the inability of traditional (print-biased) historical research methods to deal with the materials of television. In reference to the presidential campaign of 1964, Barnouw discusses the problem:[22]

> *Most books on campaigns have discussed and quoted speeches and press statements as though they were the campaign. Such materials have been readily available for quotation—campaign films, on the other hand, have not been available in libraries, and in any case they raise the question of what to quote. Television films and spots have thus eluded traditional scholarship procedures and have tended to be ignored. But the candidates in 1964 clearly considered them of key importance.*

Fortunately, Barnouw himself has provided impressive proof that such problems are not insurmountable. His masterful three-volume *History of Broadcasting in the United States* demonstrates how such materials can be effectively utilized.[23]

The single point which emerges most strongly from Barnouw's history is the degree to which the development of television, and of radio before it, has been intertwined with the politics of the country. Barnouw believes, and argues that those who govern the country also believe, that what is shown on television and how it is shown directly affects the outlook of the American people. Interestingly, he also argues that the content of "entertainment" programs is at least as important as that of commentaries, news or advertising in influencing attitudes and values. As a result, control of television has social and political consequences which go far beyond the parameters which can be measured in economic terms.

A second and more recent historical work also makes a strong case for the powerful influence of television. Daniel J. Boorstin's *The Americans: The Democratic Experience* portrays television as one of a series of inventions which have levelled and "democratized" the quality of life in America.[24] Boorstin sees all of these innovations—which include the automobile, air conditioning, the movies, mechanized farming, pre-packaged foods—as examples of the successful application of "flow technology" to mass production and mass marketing. The result was the creation of a society in which nearly everyone has more, but in which individual differences which distinguish different regions, ethnic groups, and social classes have been diminished. Television represents the culmination of this process, for it provides not merely the mass production of things but of experience itself. This commodity has proved so intoxicating, Boorstin believes, that what Arnheim had predicted 40 years earlier has come to pass: "Television watching became an addiction comparable only to life itself."

Neither Boorstin nor Barnouw offer "proof" or even much specific evidence for their assertions. The kinds of effects which they attribute to television may be of enormous importance, but they are difficult to measure or quantify. And as a society we are skeptical of what cannot be quantified. Nonetheless, the insight and perspective of the historian deserve greater attention, while empirical research continues to make its slow progress.

Television as a Cultural Force

Lord Reith, the first Chairman of the British Broadcasting Corporation, had an elegantly simple criterion for judging the worth of a program to be broadcast: did the program "say 'yes' to life"? If the answer was affirmative, he would approve. Lord Reith obviously knew what his standard meant, and he was in a position to enforce his judgements.

More recently, the British have changed their view of the role of television. The Pilkington Commission, which was established a decade ago to conduct a thorough study of television in England, concluded that the duty of broadcasting "is not to give the public what someone thinks is good for it, but rather to respect the public's right to choose from the widest possible range of subject matter and so to enlarge worthwhile experience."

In America, the issue is more complex. We have no Lord Reith (we would certainly not know what to do with him if we did); nor does the statement of the Pilkington Commission bear much relevance to American commercial television. As we have seen, in this country economic considerations have dominated in the determination of programming. Of course, economic considerations have cultural consequences: Since programs must reach as many viewers as possible, they must be designed to appeal—as much as possible—to everyone. The cultural product of such a system will inevitably be mass culture.

Much of the debate over the cultural significance of American television has essentially been a debate over the value of mass culture. A classic statement of the case against mass culture is contained in an essay written in 1953 by Dwight MacDonald. According to his definition, mass culture is distinguished by the fact that "it is solely and directly an article of mass consumption, like chewing gum ... it is fabricated by technicians hired by business; its audiences are passive consumers, their participation limited to the choice of buying or not buying."[25] Mass culture is a great leveller, incorporating genuine individual creativity into a standardized, homogenized and universally marketable product. Although it is not particularly noxious in itself (like chewing gum), MacDonald argues, the danger of mass culture is that by its superabundance it threatens to swamp the traditional distinctions between high culture and folk culture—and ultimately to destroy them. It co-opts artists by offering them fame and great monetary reward; the immediate gratification it provides erodes the potential audiences for more demanding fare.

MacDonald's essay touches on television only as one means for the dissemination of mass culture. *Television's Impact on American Culture*, published in 1956, is a collection of essays which examine the medium itself from a perspective similar to MacDonald's.[26] The authors (who are mostly educators) conclude that television had already proved itself incapable of providing a satisfactory level of excellence in its programming: Drama survives only as soap opera; intellectual accomplishment is acceptable only as a trivial quiz show performance; serious educational material is relegated to the least desirable time periods; even public affairs receives minimal attention. Given these limitations, the authors agree, a strong non-commercial alternative service is needed if American culture is to be adequately served. (The alternative to commercial television at that point consisted of a handful of educational stations struggling to broadcast a few hours of programming each day.)

While the aims of *Television's Impact* are laudable, the book falls short of living up to its title. The book is primarily a brief for strengthening noncommercial television. The authors merely point out the failure of commercial television rather than examining and evaluating its offerings in any detail. The book provides a good deal of information about the structure of the television system but very little about the products of that system. As a result, it fails to come to grips with the actual experience of watching television.

The most serious limitation of the book is that it conceives of "culture" as something which exists apart from television—something that resides in places like museums, theaters, and, above all, schools and universities. For better or worse, commercial television has become an inseparable component of American culture. Sociologist Harold Wilensky has provided clear empirical evidence for the extent to which this is true. Having investigated patterns of media use, he concludes: [27]

> ✻ There is little doubt from my data as well as others' that educated strata—even products of graduate and professional schools—are becoming full participants in mass culture; they spend reduced fractions of time in exposure to quality print and film. This trend extends to the professors, writers, artists, scientists—the keepers of high culture themselves—and the chief culprit is . . . TV.

If these findings are correct, then the issue of the content of television is not a matter of judging "what is good for the masses," but of understanding the critical role played by television in defining and expressing our culture. We need a better understanding of the context television creates—for all of us. We need to know more about what it tells us about ourselves and the world we inhabit. We need to examine what television has contributed to the ancient traditions of story and drama. We need, most of all, to develop standards appropriate to the medium to enable us to make the kind of discriminations that are the essence of the critical process.

Unfortunately, there is virtually no serious television criticism in this country today. While there are now hundreds, probably thousands, of books of film criticism—collections of reviews, studies of individual directors of various film genres, historical studies, and theoretical works—I have been able to find only a tiny handful of books of American television criticism. There is a great deal written about television; virtually every newspaper carries a television column, and many magazines pay occasional attention to the medium. But the status of television writers within journalism is generally low, and the critical study of television has no place at all in the academic world (as film did not until quite recently). Of course there are obvious reasons why this is so, some of which were suggested earlier: much of the programming is low in quality, the amount of programming is almost overwhelming, and programs vanish as soon as they are broadcast (although many popular series seem to live on indefinitely through syndication).

A book like Michael Arlen's *Living Room War*, however, demonstrates that serious television criticism is possible.[28] The pieces collected in this book (they were written originally for the *New Yorker* in 1966-1969) retain their interest even though most programs discussed have long since disappeared. As his title suggests, Arlen's principle interest was in the way the story of the Vietnam War was conveyed to America by television. Other pieces cover a range of subjects from children's programs to sports to public television. What gives them their value is that Arlen, like any good critic, attempts to place a specific program into a larger context of meaning and value, and to reach some conclusions about the state of the medium and the society it reflects.

Since *Living Room War* was published six years ago, no other critical works of similar quality have appeared. We still lack a robust, continuing discussion of what is appearing on our television screens. There are a few signs of improvement—Arlen has resumed writing his column in the *New Yorker;* last year Ron Powers of the *Chicago Sun Times* received the first Pulitzer Prize given to a newspaper television critic; and a number of other newspapers have recently hired promising young television writers—but most Americans still have no access to intelligent critical responses to the medium that pervades their lives.

If this review has presented an accurate sampling of the literature of television, it suggests that the task of understanding television as a social and cultural force has barely begun. The literature does contain much that is useful; it leaves little doubt that the impact of the medium has been massive. But the literature raises many more questions than it answers. Most striking are first, the continuing gap between what has been asserted about television's effects and what has been established by empirical research; and second, the paucity of criticism which treats television as a significant aspect of American culture. The agenda of work remaining to be done is long and challenging.

I would like to conclude with two comments that seem to me to offer fresh approaches to these problems. The first concerns television as a cultural force. It comes from the English scholar and critic, Richard Hoggart, who (like Tony Schwartz) believes that new categories are needed to properly evaluate the performance of a new medium:[29]

> *Perhaps we should stop talking about "mass culture," since the phrase invites us to stick to the old categories. Perhaps we should speak about "synthetic culture" or "processed culture"—and then remind ourselves that our job is to separate the Processed from the Living at (to use the old grading) all "levels".*
>
> *Processed culture never imagines an individual—only masses, typical audiences, status groups. Living culture, even if many people are*

enjoying it at the same time, speaks to individuals or to genuine communities, and cuts across boundaries of age or class or status. Processed culture has its eye always on the audience, the consumers, the customers. Living culture has its eye on the subject, the material. It expects the same attention to the subject from the members of its audience. Processed culture asks: "What will they take? Will this get most of them?" Living culture asks: "What is the truth of this experience and how can I capture it?"

We have to distinguish between life, creative life, and death, a mechanically-twitching death. "Life" may show itself in "serious" or "light" programmes, as scepticism or irony, or as broad emotion or firm intelligence—but will always be disinterested and honest. "Death" may show itself as trivial and slick (even though it may be purporting to be serious), cynical, against the mind and afraid of the heart—but will always be interested and out to persuade. We have to ask: Is this really a comedy? Or documentary? Or variety show? Or discussion? Or religious programme? Or is it going through the motions, a well-packaged emptiness?

The second is a statement dealing with television as a social force made by the sociologist Robert K. Merton at an Aspen Institute Television Workshop in January, 1974. To a question about the possibility of reconciling the approaches of the humanist and the social scientist to television, Merton responded:

There is no great difficulty in principle in establishing a bridge between humanistic perspectives on communications and social science perspectives. What has been absent are the bridge builders, both as individuals and as an institutionalized arrangement. But failures of the past don't necessarily mean failures in the future. . . .

Whatever the perspectives of the humanists, if you take all those that appear in print somewhere, it is in principle possible to take from those the questions, the problems, the assertions, the interpretations, the demands, the expectations, and the conceptions concerning television . . . These materials can then be carefully examined for their explicit and implicit hypotheses in order to see how the cold-blooded, dull, pedestrian activity called social science research might bear upon these imaginative, interesting, profound, and wide-sweeping perceptions.

The object is not a confrontation between humanistic and social scientific perspectives, but a translation—so that any of the ideas can be inspected with the question, can this be fruitfully investigated with the limited repertoire and with all the constraints of social science? It's not a utopian suggestion. It's a very earthy and realistic one.

Footnotes

1. *Daniel Boorstin,* The Americans: The Democratic Experience. *New York: Random House, 1973.*

2. *Rudolf Arnheim, "A Forecast of Television,"* in Film as Art. *Berkeley and Los Angeles: University of California Press, 1969.*

3. *Edgar Felix,* Television: Its Methods and Uses. *New York: McGraw-Hill, 1931.*

4. *"How Illiterate Can Television Make Us?"* Commonweal, *November 19, 1948.*

   "Television: Boon or Bane?" Public Opinion Quarterly, *Fall 1946.*

   "TV: A Mixed Blessing," American Mercury, *December 1954.*

   "Hypnosis in the Livingroom," Readers' Digest, *April 1949*

   "Video Slavery," Americas, *August 1955.*

5. *Frank V. Cantwell and Katherine F. Ruttinger, "Some Observations on the Social Effects of Television,"* Public Opinion Quarterly, *Summer 1949.*

6. *Leo Bogart,* The Age of Television. *New York: Fredrick Ungar, 1956, 1972. (The second edition contains a particularly useful bibliography updated to 1972.)*

   Two later books assessing viewer attitudes toward television are:

   Gary Steiner, The People Look at Television. *New York: Alfred A. Knopf, 1963; and*

   Robert T. Bower, Television and the Public. *New York: Holt, Rinehart and Winston, Inc., 1973.*

7. *Joseph T. Klapper,* The Social Effects of Mass Communications. *New York: The Free Press, 1960.*

8. *Harry Skornia,* Television and Society. *New York: McGraw-Hill, 1965.*

9. *Nicholas Johnson,* How to Talk Back to Your Television Set. *Boston: Little, Brown and Company, 1970.*

   Les Brown, Televi$ion: The Business Behind the Box. *New York: Harcourt Brace Jovanovich, 1971.*

10. *Fred Friendly,* Due to Circumstances Beyond Our Control. *New York: Random House, 1967.*

11.   *Roger G. Noll, Merton J. Peck, and John J. McGowan,* Economic
         Aspects of Television Regulation. *Washington: The Brookings Insti-
         tution, 1973.*

         Edward J. Epstein, News from Nowhere. *New York: Random
         House, 1973.*

12.   *Marshall McLuhan,* Understanding Media: The Extensions of Man.
         New York: McGraw-Hill, 1964.

13.   *See Toby Goldberg, "A Selective Bibliography of the Writings of and
         about Marshall McLuhan,"* Journal of Broadcasting, *Spring 1968.*

         *For a sampling of the debate about his ideas, see: Raymond Rosen-
         thal, ed.,* McLuhan: Pro and Con. *Baltimore: Penguin Books, 1969.*

14.   *Tony Schwartz,* The Responsive Chord. *Garden City, N.Y.: Anchor
         Press/Doubleday, 1973.*

15.   *Godwin C. Chu and Wilbur Schramm,* Learning from Television:
         What the Research Says. *Washington: National Association of Educa-
         tional Broadcasters, 1967.*

16.   *For a summary of the effectiveness of* Sesame Street, *see Gerald
         Lesser,* Children and Television: Lessons from Sesame Street. *New
         York: Random House, 1974.*

17.   Television and Social Behavior *(Vols. I-V). Washington: Department
         of Health, Education, and Welfare, 1972.*

18.   *The Surgeon General's Scientific Adivsory Committee on Television
         and Social Behavior,* Television and Growing Up: The Impact of
         Televised Violence. *Washington: Government Printing Office, 1972.*

19.   *For a description of the workings of the Surgeon General's Commit-
         tee and an analysis of its findings, see Douglass Cater and Stephen
         Strickland,* TV Violence and the Child: The Evolution and Fate of
         the Surgeon General's Report. *New York, The Russell Sage Founda-
         tion, 1975.*

20.   *For a comprehensive summary of the present state of knowledge
         about television and children, see Robert M. Liebert, John M. Neale,
         and Emily S. Davidson,* The Early Window: Effects of Television on
         Children and Youth. *New York: Pergamon Press, 1973.*

21.   *A project at the Rand Corporation under the direction of George
         Comstock is attempting to summarize all relevant research to date
         on "the social effects of television." Published results of the project
         should be available later in 1975.*

22.   *Erik Barnouw,* The Image Empire. *New York: Oxford University
         Press, 1970.*

23.   *The three volumes are:* A Tower in Babel *(1966),* The Golden Web
         (1968), and The Image Empire *(1970), all published by the Oxford*

University Press. *The first volume covers the history of broadcasting to 1933; the second from 1933 to 1953; the third from 1953 up to the time of writing.*

24.   *Boorstin,* op. cit.

25.   *Dwight Mac Donald, "A Theory of Mass Culture," in Alan Casty, ed.,* Mass Media and Mass Man. *New York: Holt, Rinehart and Winston, 1968.*

26.   *William Y. Eliot (ed.),* Television's Impact on American Culture. *East Lansing: Michigan State University Press, 1956.*

27.   *Harold Wilensky, "Mass Society and Mass Culture: Interdependence or Independence?"* American Sociological Review, *Vol. 29, No. 2, April 1964.*

28.   *Michael Arlen,* Living Room War. *New York: The Viking Press, 1969.*

29.   *Richard Hoggart, "Culture: Dead and Alive," in* Speaking to Each Other. *Volume I: About Society. Harmondsworth, Middlesex, England: Penguin Books, 1973.*

I submit that in grappling with the question of quality and truth in television we're grappling with questions that have obsessed us for the longest time since these belong to the province of the enlightened critic. . . . In order to make value judgments properly, we have to take very seriously the whole tradition of true criticism. How can we inject that quality of criticism, of value judgment, into a field that quite obviously has not as yet penetrated very far into such questions? Yet, if criticism is valid for the arts, it also must be valid for television as it is for life itself.

Julius Bloom

The Viewer's Experience: Notes on TV Criticism and Public Health

Benjamin DeMott

This paper argues for what nobody, presumably, would oppose—a well-informed and socially concerned criticism of television. Its chief assumption is that since TV is the paramount mass medium, with potentially momentous effect on the quality of social life, critical commentary should conjoin traditional aesthetico-moral perspectives with the results of research on response—with evidence concerning themes presented to viewers of individual programs. The primary business of the paper is to review and evaluate a more-or-less forgotten journalistic controversy that followed the introduction by the networks, a few years ago, of a new style of "realistic" situation comedy. The purpose of this review is to clarify my sense of the need for the criticism I advocate.

Since the squabble in question took place in the press, it is proper to acknowledge at the outset that journalists and Sunday supplement editors have no monopoly on extravagant, overgeneralized, underqualified chat about TV. Everyone shoots from the hip at the Tube: all professionals, regardless of field, consider their expertise a useful base for pronouncements. The theologian rushes to invoke a vocabulary of grace, perdition and sacrament, defining TV-watching as a religious experience.

> *TV shows . . . seethe with myths and heroes. They guide decisions, inform perception, provide examples of conduct. Does that make our mass-media culture 'religious'? I do not think we can explain its grip on people in any other way. Its preachers tell us what our transgression is: our armpits are damp, our breath is foul, our wash is gray, our car is inadequate. They hold up models of saintly excel-*

Benjamin DeMott is Professor of English at Amherst and a columnist for the *Atlantic Monthly*.

*lence before our eyes: happy, robust, sexually appreciated people
who are free, adventurous, competent, attractive. These blessed ones
have obviously been saved or are well on the way. And the sacra-
mental means of grace that have lifted them from perdition are available to you and me—soaps, deodorants, clothes, pills, cars. If, despite
our devoted attendance at the sacraments, we never seem to attain
the promised bliss, well, salvation can be the question of a lifetime.
Mass-media culture is a religion, and we rarely get out of its temple.*
(Harvey Cox, The Seduction of the Spirit, *1973*)

This writer's hostility to commercials is bracing—but does his account of TV as
anxiety-creator square with facts of feeling? I myself am inclined to think of TV
as a holiday world, one in which I master the revels, proof against any
intimidation. Harried elsewhere by manners (mustn't interrupt), or by the
obligation of response (look attentive, repeat after me, remember, tell me what
you think), I am, before the box, a figure of command: I (and my pre-teen child
as well) flip the dial cavalierly, laying waste to images, ripping off multitudes
beyond counting, cutting the President himself dead in mid-sentence if we
choose. The force of divinity in this setting, in other words, doesn't seem to me
to be an anxiety-producing commercial message; instead it is nothing other than
the energy of my abrupt, unapologetic, finger-flipping rudeness. Should not the
possibility that others besides myself fail to experience television as moral
torment figure in theological comment?

      Or again, here is an architect philosophizing on TV newscasters,
claiming that these people are mere sounds, a sum of inhuman noise comparable
to that made by car engines:

*With television it is not the program that is important, certainly not
the substance of the news. It is the* sound, *the background blur of
voices that like the ticking of a clock or the cyclic 'ping' of sonar is
only significant when it changes, or when it stops . . . The droning
voice, night after night, week after week, resembles the noise of a car
engine.(Martin Pawley,* The Private Future, *1974)*

Can I adjust such talk to my feeling for Walter Cronkite, companionable
chronicler of my own and my family's dailiness? Suppose this "image" exists for
me as a "round" character, a central figure in an interesting human drama,
someone whose nature, opinions, feelings I piece together, night after night, in a
manner not wholly different from that in which, as I imagine, the Victorian
reader of the Victorian novel worked his or her way into intimacy with hero or
heroine as the "serial parts" came forth: am I to understand myself as pure
eccentric? I note Walter's firm but comfortable relationships with his

juniors—Dan, Roger, Marvin, Connie and the rest. Each of the younger ones finishes his piece on this or that Special Committee event by deferentially, goodhumoredly repeating Walter's name—Walter? Listening, I grasp that my "newscaster" is no harsh taskmaster, is easy, relaxed, prepared to value the pride of the young, heartened by their abilities, and, as well, by their maturing claims to independence, living space, respect. I note too that this same Walter himself possesses an elder: just now I catch him engaged with an overhead monitor, listening soberly and admiringly to Eric Sevareid. Well. Naturally I understand that Walter is concerned for his cue, and I do not tell myself that he accepts each word from Mr. Sevareid as gospel. Yet I feel Walter's constant awareness of Mr. Sevareid's dignity and solidity and importance: I know he counts this whitehaired man as a valuable elder. And now Walter is telling me of an extraordinary event in Sarasota—a TV person like himself, a woman newscaster, has attempted suicide with a handgun *while on camera.* Walter's manner assures me that he would prefer not to have to report such an event, assures me that he believes I understand that while he lodges sometimes with weirdos, he's not truly of the hysterical masscom world. The point is simply that here is a strange and "newsworthy" happening, and what can he do but tell me about it? Some in his audience, not myself but some, would feel cheated had he not put in this hateful picture. And now Walter is talking to me about Alan Shepherd, the astronaut, who's retiring from the Navy at fifty to take up work in a Houston construction company. As it happens, I know that Walter is a friend of Shepherd's and I sense him registering this retirement as a milestone of a sort. The event matters to Walter; as he recounts it I sense him inwardly wishing an old buddy well and assuming that I too have the same generous impulse: here is a journey's ending, a passage of years. And now it is time for his salute: Walter winds the day down for me, turning his hands up unprotestingly. The world is a place to be sighed at, smiled at; it's something to cope with, we'll tell you, nothing to be trivialized—yet let us be reconciled. There is humor too. "And that's the way it is."

Each day I feel I know him better from within, guessing him out, intuiting approval, disapproval, shock. Someone reports—in a tone of wonder—that I and the majority of Americans trust him more than any other public figure. And I think, why wonder? Which public figure—except those characters in Dickens' novels a century and more ago—can I or my contemporaries know so well? Who could be so asinine or blank about human response to imagine that I hear this man as noise? Is he not the rarity of my world: Someone *Known?*

To repeat: the swift dramatic figure or image purporting to lay bare the essence of this or that viewing experience seldom seems to me commensurate with the nature of that experience. But once again I must emphasize that my comment on Cox or Pawley, like the comment on the newspaper battle below, isn't meant to chide individuals. The aim is to clarify areas of incertitude and to press a case for the employment of new resources to help us discover where, in relation to this medium, we truly are.

On to the conflict. It began with a Sunday *Times* polemic by the novelist Laura Hobson laying out the hero of *All in the Family* for making bigotry lovable. Ms. Hobson's attack on Archie Bunker brought in its train reams of response—letters from script writers, TV directors, pop-culture watchers (Nat Hentoff), poets (Muriel Rukeyser), leaders of the B'nai Brith Anti-Defamation League, schoolteachers, concerned parents and citizens. The show's producer, Norman Lear, added his own voice to the throng, praising Archie as a victory over stereotypes of the bigot and hailing Lear as "lovable myself." During the 1971-2 season *All in the Family* ranked as the number one sitcom, reaching 40 million households and 100 million probable viewers. Print media editors were disposed to keep the subject alive for a time. *Newsweek, Life,* and several other journals ran cover stories on Archie, complete with punditry on what it all meant. But neither they nor anyone else, of course, could prevent the subject from fading, like most media sensations, rather rapidly.

As might be guessed, the principals in the argument adhered throughout to a strategy of disputation—motive-maligning—that is unproductive of moral illumination. Ms. Hobson raged that *All in the Family* masked the ugliness of bigotry:

> *Had Norman Lear never realized [she asked] that what bigots really called Jews was kike or sheeny? That they didn't really go around talking about the chosen people or one of that tribe or yenta? That their own words, the words they actually used, were kike and sheeny? Then why did Norman Lear, in this honest portrayal of the bigot next door, never say either?*

Implied answer: because Lear was secretly in favor of prejudice, at least as it manifests itself in the American underclasses.

Lear countered in kind: why was Ms. Hobson undisturbed about the vocabulary of upperclass ethnic slurs (schwarz and the like)? Implied answer: the lady looked with sympathy on Establishment-style bigotry. Moral oneupmanship, the determination to pin harsh labels on the opposition, the belief that all squabbles ultimately reduce to one question (which of us is evil?)—these forces made for an animated quarrel and encouraged other combatants to speak in even fiercer tones of protestation than those with which the tiff began. They didn't, however, define or clarify major issues, or point a direction for those whose job it was to deal with the adjacent life-problems.

Then, as now, speaking of "issues" and "social policies" in connection with Archie Bunker passes a cloud of solemnity over an experience which to millions, to tens of millions, seems deliciously issue-free. Night after night Archie slams through his doorway, heavy with workday-subway miseries—but the miseries vanish fast. Here's his armchair, here's his *News,* his cigar, the thought of a beer later at Kelsey's. . . . It won't do to claim that Archie's TV living room is a holiday world for him; irascibility and exacerbation have a place in it, people need to be set straight, challenges have to be met. But it's a fact that for Archie these confrontations are some kind of a ball. Whatever the constraints of on-the-job, dog-eat-dog habituality, at home the man is free and various—by turns a mimic, a stand-up funnyman, an instructor, a voice of military command, omnipotence itself. And for the audience the sense of Archie's *enjoying* himself is strong and vivid. He will get it in the end, no doubt: one or another plot turn shows him up in the last few frames. But when it happens it happens so swiftly that you barely catch him bewildered, much less depressed. And before the switcheroo, what satisfactions! Sly, knowing, fleering, mocking, teasing, daring, contradicting, Archie *runs a show.* He rips off a thousand gags, announcing he's got his hormones on a leash and that his son-in-law Mike's friend makes Mike look like a pile of inner tubes. When Mike tells him beauty is in the eye of the beholder, Archie has the kicker—stupid is in the eye of the Polack. Home from a sexy flick he explains he had to watch it TILT, crick-necked, nobody on screen was ever standing up. Tell him he ought to face this or that problem, be realistic, etc., that trouble "of this kind" is part of life, and he tells you so is throwing up, but he doesn't want to look at it. Tell him he ought to celebrate because his daughter and son-in-law have been "with us man and wife" for a year and he answers that this would be like celebrating the 365th day of a toothache. What is a homosexual dentist? A tooth fairy, says Arch. Why are the Mexicans great fighters? Because, says Arch, with sixteen in a family they've got to kill each other for chow. Then beyond all this come the big words, the fancy words—inedibly for indelibly, epaulets for epithets, suppository for derogatory, invading for evading—spoken always with a brio that practically demands the viewer to believe that Arch not only recognizes the malapropisms but invented each one himself.

And far more important, time and again he confirms his estimate of his worth. Around him stand ranks of dimwits, but Archie knows and knows. Miles off he smells a racket—insurance estimates, repair bills, package deals from your friendly undertaker (guaranteed against "washout"), live-in gigs cooked up by wifey and his hairy son-in-law, come-ons from vanity song publishers, this week's pieties about Watergate, change-your-name hokum à la "the Hebes." And Archie knows the uses and value of his expertise. He knows that if it weren't for the likes of him the food on tonight's table—call it Chink chow or Chinese, plain fruit or cling peaches—wouldn't be there, and maybe not the country either. And this hearth-knowledge, hearth-confidence, is, by and large, enlivening. It rouses him to a thousand expressive bits—passages of faking and mugging, endlessly winking over the cables at fifty million fellow husbands; it lifts him to a nimble, wordy, eye-popping zaniness; it makes him, through the agency of Carroll O'Connor, first of all a *card,* a figure of frolic. For openers a song with dingbat Edith. Thereafter, at many a turn in many a segment the action moves toward minstrelsy—as in the show about the black thieves who let the Bunkers off because Edith charms them. And always such movement *feels* imminent, because Archie's personal tone, the goodtime-showbiz ambiance surrounding him, not only permits but encourages it.

Therefore it's not the easiest trick in the world—thinking about Archie Bunker in connection with issues, lessons, problems, social policy and the like. Still it *was* sensible of Ms. Hobson to bring up issues, and it remains so today. The problem is that while all the major theses in dispute in the Archie controversy had, and continue to have, important social bearings, and while it's feasible to test out each in a way that would go far to prove or disprove it, neither then nor now can they be "settled" at any level save that of opinion. To put it more flatly: issues that should have been debated soberly, directly, with assurance of achieving sound knowledge, were and are debated in a context dense with superstition, ignorance, and an incapacity to advance beyond myths.

What exactly were the areas of dispute? One had to do with the processes of moral education—that is to say, with the problem of effective teaching in the field of ethical relations among men. Ms. Hobson was absolutely confident that she understood the process of moral education, and on the basis of this understanding she placed *All in the Family* as the first television program:

> ... to teach impressionable children that they're not wanted in
> certain neighborhoods, that there's something that makes people
> laugh at them and look down on them and call them names ... that
> it's quite all right to go around saying spade and Hebe and coon and
> spic—for of course kids always imitate what they see on TV ...

The Anti-Defamation League spokesman, Benjamin Epstein, was equally confident, and he agreed with Ms. Hobson:

> We do not believe that it is possible to combat bigotry by laughing
> at a central bigoted figure who evokes the sympathy of the audience.
> We feel the show sanctions the use of derogatory epithets. When the
> program is over the listener has had a good time and he has enjoyed
> the bigotry of Archie rather than feeling a sense of revulsion.

Mr. Lear, for his part, was no less confident of his grasp of the processes of moral education. But he considered that the educational effect of *All in the Family* was precisely opposite to the one described by Hobson-Epstein:

> *. . . when army bases and Fair Housing Congresses and church*
> *groups ask for copies of our shows for use in their interracial pro-*
> *grams, or when the Western Electric Company makes the same re-*
> *quest for use among its 22,000 employees, you can be sure their*
> *intention is not to have people sitting around, pencil in hand, wait-*
> *ing for the epithets to fly. The intention is to have thousands of*
> *employees, white and black, Jew and Gentile, laugh together.*

What can be said about this difference except that all parties are working in relative darkness? What is more apparent than that all accounts of the moral consequences of this program were and remain simplistic? Men have been aware for years of the uselessness of lectures on "goodness" and "right conduct." John Dewey himself, a passionate believer in moral education, warned off educators from speechmaking about ethics, proposing a distinction between abstract preaching about morality and demonstrations of the ways in which moral ideas take effect in conduct—efforts to transform these ideas into *"moving ideas, motive forces in the guidance of conduct."* Certainly it's possible that a successful exposition of the context of prejudice might qualify as a demonstration of the way in which moral ideas take effect in conduct. Often the majority culture congratulates itself for flattering the minority culture about some marginal achievement—witness Archie explaining to Lionel, his son-in-law's black friend, that blacks invariably make better athletes because they can "run faster and jump higher and don't bruise so easy." Conceivably this dramatization of "friendly behavior" as in fact a mode of condescension could breed deeper comprehension of bias, an alertness to forms the virus takes in me that might otherwise go unnoticed. The same can be said about "general good-natured" laughter at cruel epithets: it's possible for moral instruction to flow from a sequence of events suggesting that since stupid people alone are inclined to say such words the words must be meaningless—comical, like a rabbit's foot or other charm, empty of force. But it's quite as conceivable that the processes might work in another way. Yet while it was feasible to seek out solid knowledge about how they do work, no effort toward that end was set in motion then and none has since been proposed.

A second area of darkness was, roughly, aesthetic, having to do with the psychology of comic action. Nietzsche said "jokes are the epitaphs of emotion"; Ms. Hobson quoted Bergson on "the absence of feeling that usually accompanies laughter . . . Comedy . . . begins in a growing callousness . . . an unavowed intention to humiliate." And the conventional hostile argument held that Archie's mockery of minorities induced in the mass audience a suspension of feeling for those minorities, a "growing callousness." The conventional defense held that Archie is a *losing* mocker: he repeatedly defeats himself. It's undeniable that Archie is often mocked—as a misuser of language, an over-suspicious man, a Puritan shocked by his daughter's willingness to say the word "breasts" out loud. And since, as indicated, Archie too is made fun of, might it not follow that audiences experience a "growing callousness" toward him, as well as to the victims of his racism? People laugh when Archie invokes this or that stereotype of the black man, while talking with Lionel: why doesn't the laughter humiliate Archie? People laugh when Archie chides his son-in-law as a "meathead Polack" for trusting an artist friend not to touch his wife, even though she's posing nude for the man. Does that laughter mean that Archie is perceived as "defeating" himself, or is the response more complicated? Perhaps Mike's gullibility appears too trustful—beamish or sentimental or worse—and therefore Archie's chiding is heard as a voice of wisdom? There was no end of super-confident talk about these matters at the time—but again no basis for confidence on either side.

And the same can be said about yet another problem area, that concerning the question: Who, in class terms, truly gets the joke about Archie? Many commentators claimed that while well-fixed exurbanites probably saw Archie Bunker "as an ill-educated boob who constantly revealed his lower-classness by spouting stuff like 'misconscrued idea,' 'detergent to crime,' 'I'm mortifried,' and 'not German to the conversation,' " this is essentially an "elitist point of view"—nothing that can be shared, as Ms. Hobson wrote, by the bulk of "the 100 million viewers who aren't college graduates and executives..." Producer Lear gave the predictable answer, namely that Ms. Hobson was a snob, that her argument "raised the age-old specter of the intellectuals' mistrust of the lower middle classes," that she herself was anti-democratic, etc. But again what authority underlay the accusations? They neither confirmed nor refuted that class and education levels affect perceptions of the hero of *All in the Family.*

In sum: three areas of dispute, much ferocity, zero illumination. Nobody knew whether the Hobsons or the Lears or their successors in the dispute down to the present—the teach-by-silence faction or the teach-by-confrontation faction—were right. All that's become clear is that if the former were correct, incalculable social damage has been done in this country week by week, for enormous profit, and that if the latter were correct, a profoundly important opening toward moral education for a mass audience has been obscured in a murk of piety and superstition.

If there were serious uncertainties about how to proceed toward clarification, the situation as it stands would be excusable. But in fact sound lines of approach have been visible since long before the program in question scored its popular triumph. *All in the Family* was and remains a profit-making venture, hugely successful. A portion of its profits should be spent on an inquiry aimed at lighting up the dark areas just specified. At least a half-dozen research centers in the country could develop a research design sophisticated enough to yield if not hard knowledge, then invaluable clues to the social consequences of the Archie shows. (Among the organizations are the National Opinion Research Center at Chicago University, the Survey Research Centers at the Universities of Michigan and California [Berkeley], and the Bureau for Applied Social Research at Columbia.) These organizations have cadres of interviewers adept at handling complex, "class cross-section" interviewing problems. Most have records of research in special branches of the ecology of tolerance that go back two and three decades and that testify to familiarity with the kinds of variables—psychic, political, economic, sexual, situational—that inevitably figure in such research. Given the existing resources, experience, and capabilities, it is astonishing that no person or agency—not the Anti-Defamation League, not the author of *Gentleman's Agreement,* not *Commentary* magazine, not Ralph Nader—ever issued a call for their use in the *All in the Family* case.

And it's the more astonishing when you consider that the demand that the media accept responsibility for financing inquiry into the social consequences of their changing inventions has been heard in industry circles before. During the Berkeley Centennial several years ago, editors, Justice Department officials, the director of program development for Westinghouse Broadcasting Company and the president of NET met on this very subject—prejudice, the media, and media responsibility—under the sponsorship of the Rockefeller Foundation. The panel raised such matters as the "whitening" of blacks in the popular situation comedies and drama of that day. ("Doesn't the breakdown of prejudice require that the white man come to recognize and feel discomforted about what it really means to be black in a white society—to be rejected, to be hurt, to be treated as an object? And doesn't it require that we come to acknowledge and respect the real differences in values and life style?")

More to the present point, the panel came down hard on the need for research into the social effects of new dramatic or other styles before programs enbodying them are nationally aired. Summarizing the discussion, Dore Schary wrote:

> The public is amazingly complacent about the media's trying
> out all sorts of strategies that might drastically affect the quality of
> social life without demanding to know what that effect might be. A
> pharmaceutical house cannot release a new drug on the market
> without first subjecting it to rigorous tests; yet the public evidently
> finds social illnesses far less threatening than physical illnesses, or it
> feels that social ills are just too big and too complex to be dealt with
> rationally. Until public pressure mounts, the media may continue to
> plead innocent until proved guilty.

Admittedly, sociological inquiry has limits. ("No public opinion poll," David Riesman once wrote, "no matter how large or how imaginatively stratified the sample, turns up enough cases or data to answer to questions its results raise.... Polls are detective stories in which the reader must supply essential clues.") And admittedly every human being has one or more areas of response in which intuition speaks so strongly as to dismiss out of hand the notion that, at least on this particular turf, any need for research actually exists. I suggested earlier how my intuitions conflicted with a theologian's and an architect's. I can add here that I am quite deeply persuaded of the accuracy of my perception of the way in which upper-middle-class viewers orient themselves toward Archie. Is it not "obvious" that, whether or not Archie is lovable, he is presented in a manner that seduces his social superiors into congratulating themselves on their sophistication, style, and learning? What person who has risen socially and has spent a part of his lifetime among the elite can have failed to notice the extraordinary complacency of the rich with regard to their own advantages? The rich have been taught that it's bad taste to speak or think of blacks as "inferior intelligences"—but they apply similar terms, with few inhibitions, to white hardhats, postmen and cops. Seldom does it occur to them that the base attitudes they associate with blue-collar whites have as much to do with the quality of education provided by the whole society for low-income citizens as with any "natural-born" crudity of mind. Archie defeats Archie, yes, and no one can be positive how Archie is read by his "own kind," his peers.

But I myself experience small doubt when facing the question of how his "betters" see him. In virtually every show, indeed, a moment arrives in which anger flickers in me—anger that it is so easy for the more fortunate to dissociate themselves from the vulgarity of the row-house world, to regard Archie's "defeats" and general ignorance as in no way flowing from themselves, to accept no responsibility for Archie's limitations. *Who exploits Archie's bad taste for profit in TV? Who but Ivy grads, prepared for plunder by Scarsdale High SATs? Who are the editors, reporters, copywriters who immemorially "write down" to Archie for profit, telling him salvation is bowling shoes and a Buick Riviera? Are they really incapable, these lads, of grasping that their education costs five to ten times as much as his, that their taste, flexibility, nicely developed sense of shame have far less to do with natural gifts or diligence than with the luck of the economic draw? Why do people preen themselves for correct ideas they themselves never generated in contest with their opposites, but which they merely sucked up in The Compound? What makes a corporation tax lawyer believe his "liberalism" about race is a product of personal intellectual distinction rather than a product of training in manners that practically every citizen in the country could similarly profit from if he had a comparable shot at it?*

But certainty on this model is in fact only another species of defensiveness or self-righteousness, further evidence—like the readings offered in the original squabble itself—that moving beyond conditioning, interest and learned norms of personal resentment is extremely difficult work.[1] And precisely here lie the bearings of the local case on the larger problem of a sound television criticism. I may, as critic, approve or disapprove the terms on which the father in *Apple's Way* seeks to dramatize his own respect for the law, or the terms of the contrast developed in any of a half-dozen crime shows between official law enforcement officers and private eyes, or the terms on which a minority group is "humanized" or "dignified" in *Sanford & Son* or *Shaft*. But there is a sense in which, on this turf, criticism is too important a matter to be left solely to critics. "The religion of democracy," said William James, "needs nothing so much as sympathetic interpretation to one another of the different classes of which society consists." Could the characterization of Archie Bunker qualify as "sympathetic interpretation?" Is the presence or absence of such interpretation on TV immaterial?

Absolutely immaterial, say the McLuhanists, and the latter position echoes and re-echoes in culture-critique generalizations and discourses on sacraments and noise like those mentioned above. Isolated moral protests, flareups of "concern," gestures of despair—these are ineffective at counteracting such disregard of particulars. Isolated efforts at "improving programs"—I have in mind the recent $25,000 prizes for individual TV shows offered by the Lilly Endowment—are also likely to prove inconsequential.

What is needed is a current of clarity about the nature of the dominant "moving idea" realized in the majority of households watching this or that TV product, and, in addition, new resources for its aesthetic and moral evaluation. The current of clarity I speak of should figure in all critical assessments of programs. But a foundation for criticism broader and firmer than it can provide must also be built. Daily work aimed at evaluating the media must become a norm in the classroom; so too, in election seasons, must classroom exercises in the assessment of campaign coverage. We need concrete ventures in the improvement of television criticism in the press and on TV itself. We need to produce and disseminate guidebooks for intelligent viewing—handbooks on media styles and practices suitable for the use of teachers, parents, and children. We need to draw on existing capital—it's especially rich in Britain—in the form of knowledge about teaching methods in this field that are effective for pupils in the lower schools.

We need all this because it is only by joint efforts of social scientists and humanists that the sense of mass communications entertainment as an exempt, purely private, undiscussable world can be qualified and the raising of critical consciousness can begin. McLuhanism and specialist *profundum* have joined with traditional American wariness of quarrels about "personal tastes" to kill off belief in the functions of discrimination vis-á-vis "popular favorites." Obsession with refining market research has lured minds away from the labor of discovering sound ways of probing attitudinal responses to programs as distinguished from commercials. Sniffishnessness about "pop" in the universities has inhibited responsible intellectual inquiry into TV aesthetics. The result has been the creation in contemporary life of a morally vacant continent of communication—an air in which no substantive ethical issue is allowed to breathe. (You have your view; I have mine.) The task is to find means of penetrating this amoral "purity." The health of our feeling for each other is at stake and, perhaps more than that, the future of sympathy itself.

Footnotes

1.   *It is, after all, possible that the absence of the harshest words from Archie's speech—"kike" or "nigger"—has the effect of narrowing the distance between him and educated viewers; if the worst words were used, nobody "nice" could conceivably "identify" with him, while, as it is, the door is perhaps kept slightly ajar. (The English TV drama "Till Death Do Us Part," which Mr. Lear borrowed heavily from in creating "All in the Family," employed much fiercer terms of hatred than Archie's. The effect would seem to be to exclude absolutely the possibility of an educated, right-minded viewer experiencing any feeling of solidarity with the working class blokes who spew forth ethnic slurs of that kind. And the exclusion appears appropriate for a society far more intensely conscious and accepting of class difference than ours.)*

I do not accept the concept that original and complex ideas cannot appear on TV anymore than I, or anyone else, now accepts the once prevalent belief that serious poetry can be written only in Greek and Latin. All the constraints of TV are real, but they're not conclusive unless we accept them . . . I believe the assumption has never been fully tested that it's impossible to attract a large, literate, regular audience for TV programming that uses the medium well and is concerned with ideas . . . There must be a commitment to the integrity of ideas as integral to a society's health and a commitment to the television medium as a valid way of expressing these ideas . . . Television is only what we think it is and make it.

James Kraft

Communicating Ideas by Television[1]

David Littlejohn

Almost from its beginning as a means of popular communication, television has been derided by the intellectual community. For every professional thinker who has written or spoken of its great educating and civilizing potential, there have been hundreds who professed to regard American television as barbaric, brain-softening trash: as a dangerous force working *against* serious thought, critical standards, and human values.

There seem to be fewer of them than there were a few years ago (or perhaps I now talk to different people), but American university faculties still include many television-haters who "wouldn't have one in the house," and who firmly believe they miss nothing important by not owning a set. (The television-hating intellectual, modified version, has one "only for the news," "only for PBS," or "only for the children.")

The reasons for this disdain are not difficult to figure out. The economic structure of American television has traditionally obliged its programming to be directed towards the largest possible audience, and to please, divert, and satisfy this audience as painlessly as possible. But the independent professional thinker is nobody's average man. He thrives, even in his off-hours, on more solid nourishment than his fellows, and has probably educated or refined himself to a point where he cannot tolerate a great many common pleasures.

He is likely, also, to be more aware than most viewers of the sales-conscious and cynical reasoning that underlies most of commercial

---

David Littlejohn is Associate Professor and Associate Dean of the School of Journalism, University of California at Berkeley. He is the author or editor of six books of literary criticism and biography. He has written and broadcast critical reviews for Public Television, including a 39-week national PBS series ("Critic-at-Large") in 1971-72, and presently serves as a regular book reviewer for *The New Republic*.

television. He will see not only the program, but the *purpose* of the program. He will dislike (by reason of this independence) the feeling of being manipulated, every bit as much as he will dislike (for political or other reasons) the feeling of attending so intimately to "an advertising medium occasionally interrupted by programs," a long chain of sales pitches for the products of American corporations. Even with so-called "quality" programs, this aspect of television-watching rankles many independent thinkers.

The more you know about any subject, the more a vulgarized treatment of it will reveal its shortcomings and give offense. The professional historian winces at the lying popularizations of a grade-school text; the serious journalist is wounded by local "happy talk" news. And to the educated man or woman of taste, the simplifications and popular reductivism, the shortening and sweetening of almost *all* material offered on television renders it at best inadequate, at worst intolerable. They are not for *him*, these 26-minute, every-week-at-the-same-time parcels subdivided for short attention spans (and to make room for commercial interruptions), resonantly narrated or obviously acted, brightly colored, closely focused, nervously edited—this is not the way *his* mind is disposed to receive its information or entertainment. He may well see in them what Rudolf Arnheim has called "the devaluation of the word," the destruction by apparently absolute and undebatable images of what he has always regarded as the only tool of reason. "When communication can be achieved by pointing with the finger . . . the mouth grows silent, the writing hand stops, and the mind shrinks."

He may even worry about the harm such programs are doing to other people, people less perceptive or discriminating than he. People wounded by vulgarity often believe that what hurts them must be hurting others, even if those others are too dense to be *aware* of their own internal injuries. Much of the intellectual's antagonism towards television is directed at what he regards as its substantive flaws: its distortions and trivializations, its manipulative weakening of sales resistance, its promotion of stereotypes and unthought responses in order to satisfy a hundred million viewers at once. But much of it is personal, a matter of taste and caste, like the symphony lover's uninformed disdain for more popular music, or the book lover's distrust of brightly colored, passive, public means of receiving information or enlightenment.

There are exceptions. The intransigent television-hater, as I say, seems to be rarer in the academy today than he once was. There are serious students of popular culture nowadays, and one expects them to watch (if not enjoy) all manner of illiterate drivel. I have colleagues in journalism school who try to watch all three networks' news broadcasts every night. The range of programming one may shamelessly admit to watching in intellectual circles seems to be expanding. *Masterpiece Theatre* and Kenneth Clark were always acceptable; but in 1973 one could even risk admitting to the CBS Saturday Night Lineup (*All in the Family, M.A.S.H.,* and *The Mary Tyler Moore Show*).

The discovery that your favorite physicist or philosopher yields to *one* lowbrow interest, like *Bonanza* or pro football or the funnies, is usually regarded as making him seem "human." And which of us does not know at least one closet TV-addict among serious scholars?

But the fact remains that distrust of television (and not only of television as it is, but television generally, television as a means of communication) is still the rule rather than the exception among independent professional thinkers. And the more they learn about the actual power structure and decision-making processes of American television, the greater their disdain is likely to be.

So it is not surprising that so few of them in this country have ever considered making use of television to communicate their own ideas.

And yet: television is the most thoroughly attended to, most pervasive, and probably most influential means of propagating ideas in this country today. It can be instantaneous in its reach, intimate in its reception. It can exercise the most extraordinary sensory and emotional appeal. You can find authorities who believe that it molds minds, fixes modes of perception, and determines what is thought of as desirable and even real for hundreds of millions of people.

The systems of television in leading Western countries have developed into a mass medium so unparalleled in the extent of its audience as virtually to require a redefinition of the adjective *mass*. A best-selling new book in this country may reach from 100,000 to 500,000 households in a year, a record or a paperback one or two million. The biggest newspaper in America sells two million copies a day. A concert tour or top Broadway play may attract a million spectators. Six million may buy tickets to the most successful film of the year. *Playboy* reaches seven million, *Reader's Digest* (and *TV Guide*!) eighteen million homes with every issue. But an American commercial network television program in mid-evening may be regarded as a failure—as a *failure*—if it is not watched simultaneously by at least twenty million households every week.

This power to reach and to influence may seem gloriously desirable, rich beyond the dreams of the most ambitious philosopher-king.

But does the serious thinker *want* such an audience? And can a medium designed to capture such an audience be of any use to him?

No one disputes that publication of the original ideas of critical and independent thinkers is worthwhile. Anthropologists and art historians, biologists and biographers, clergymen and critics, philosophers and pundits, political commentators and political scientists—whatever they may call themselves, those who think independently, originally, and professionally; those who *deal in ideas*—it is agreed that intelligent and thoughtful persons can benefit from the publication of their ideas. The thinkers, too, will benefit from such publication. Once exposed, their ideas can be tested and improved through the give-and-take challenge of attack and reply. Different thinkers working in the same field may discover each other, benefit each other actually or spiritually, even end up collaborating. *New* thinkers may be enlisted, encouraged, inspired.

If you believe in "Intellectual History," in a world of ideas that exists apart from those who think them, then such interaction and cross-fertilization is essential to its survival and growth. It is virtually a part of its definition.

Publication, then, yes. But publication how? And for whom?

Not necessarily indiscriminate, promiscuous, total publication—all that is implied in the metaphor "broadcasting." Communication from scholar to scholar; from original thinker to his popularizer-retailer (from research historian, for example, to teacher of history); from professional to amateur; from specialist to dilettante; from the art critic to the art lover, informed political commentator to the citizen-voter, knowledgeable journalist to interested layman. For each variety and level of useful intellectual communication one can conceive of (1) the right thinker-communicator; (2) the right audience; (3) the right approach— style, tone, length, etc.; and (4) the right medium of communication.

So where, in all this, does television fit in?

For some kinds of intellectual communication, nowhere at all. Scholarship *per se*—new thinking in any field, refined, high-level, front-line thinking—is addressed by one expert to another. It is aimed at those who can appreciate the possible value of the new thought, because they know what has been thought before. Television would be an absurdly inefficient way to reach such an audience. Serious new work, moreover, must be readily consultable, if it is to incorporate itself into the living world of ideas. It must be argued with and used by other scholars, looked up by students, footnoted, modified, revised. It must circulate to libraries in other countries; get itself translated, abstracted, indexed. This may all be possible one day for television reports, but it is not so today. Television, moreover, as it presently exists—and I will be saying more about this—encourages casual and inattentive reception, exaggerates matters irrelevant to serious thinking, drastically limits the *amount* one can either transmit or receive, and makes it impossible to go back and check over what has been said. For these and other reasons, television as we know it is never likely to be utilized for the transmission of this first and most precious level of serious thought.

Television *as we know it:* but that is the problem. The field of "Communications" has attracted many utopian futurologists whose liberated imaginations are able to contrive *better* television systems for better worlds, radically different from those we know. I will have a try at this myself, at the conclusion of this paper. But in general I am more disposed to accept the existing order of things, and to inquire how it may be well or better used.

And television as we know it includes in its makeup a great many considerations that are extraneous or irrelevant to, possibly even inimical to, the communication of serious thought. The first of these is its almost built-in obsession with the largest possible audience. And large audiences often have absolutely nothing to do with serious intellectual communication.

Commercial network "prime time" costs thousands of dollars a minute, because (a) it is so cumbersome to produce and transmit, (b) it is used as an advertising medium, and (c) it is likely to be watched by so many people. These people *expect* skillfully packaged mass entertainments on network prime time. And those who provide them with these entertainments expect them in return to keep watching, and can risk little or no diminution in the number of prospective customers for their sponsors' products.

But my experience has been that even in the off-hour and non-commercial byways of American television, ratings—that is, *audience size*—matter very, very much. The most enlightened idealist among Public Television executives would find it hard to justify producing a program, local or national, that could not be expected to reach at least a certain minimum number of homes.

"Publication," in television, is not up to the publisher. A television producer cannot declare a halt after a press run of so many copies and then distribute them carefully to the proper markets. It is up to the consumer. And there are 2.3 times as many potential customers as there are television-owning households in the United States. Many people in television are haunted by the thought of those hundred-plus million sets out there, *waiting* to be turned on. However esoteric (or awful) one's own particular program, there is just the chance that all those people will subscribe, buy the product—a chance that no print publisher ever, ever has. Just think: sixty million homes! Or even, for a local program, 96 percent of the people in that area; or even a third of them—all those people able to watch *me*, watch my station, my program. Even ten percent. Even *one* percent. "Even a 1.0 national rating delivers over 600,000 homes, nearly twice the circulation of *Harper's* and *Atlantic*" (Martin Mayer, *About Television*). All the viewers have to do is turn a switch.

Television producers and station managers don't always reach their goals, obviously, not even their one in 100. But they tend to feel ashamed if they don't. (Is *The New Yorker* unhappy reaching one American household in 120? *The New Republic* one in 300? *The Yale Review* one in 3000?)

Why this obsession with audience size, in almost all branches of TV? Partly in imitation of Prime Time. Talk of the giant network programs so dominates the television industry that the attitudes and aspirations of their producers become a model for all levels of the trade. *Broadcasting, TV Guide,* and *Variety* tend to look with pity on serious programs that achieve no more than 1. or 2. ratings (i.e., audiences of less than one million homes)—as if television's precious "air" were being wasted on any program not glowing out through at least a quarter of the available screens at a time.

An artificial competitive situation is set up, partly by rival advertisers, agencies, and networks, but also by the fact that one can only watch one television program at a time, whereas one may subscribe to twenty magazines, buy dozens of books. You can read *Time, Newsweek,* and *U.S. News,* but you cannot easily watch each edition of the ABC, CBS, and NBC evening news. You may buy six rival cookbooks, but you must decide (this season at least, early 1975) between *Macmillan and Wife, Kojak,* and *Masterpiece Theatre.* Hence the networks' mania for audience "share." Three networks yield, ideally, three-thirds of a total. 33 percent, then (or, scattering a few points among PBS and non-network affiliates, 30 percent), is one's desirable share of the sets-turned-on at any given time.[2] 35 is paradise. 25 is passable. 20 is near to failure. 15 and you probably won't be back next year. Reducing the scale, but imitating the style, Public Television crows out loud whenever it reaches five.

There are exceptions. There are whole channels in major cities (major "markets," television calls them) that never get over one or two percent, and are presumably content. Cable and pay TV will allow even smaller minorities to be viable. But even the federal, foundation, and corporate underwriters of non-commercial television, I have found, are desperately concerned about audience size—as, for that matter, is the BBC. ("I should be . . . concerned if we fell below the 40:60 proportion [of BBC to ITV viewers], because it would mean that we were either not good enough in the quality of what we were offering, or too highbrow in our general balance to retain our hold on the large audience," wrote Charles Curran, former Director-General of the BBC.) Public television station managers think in commercial network terms, use the same language. The best television professionals are anxious to be involved with high-rated shows. It is that kind of a medium. Electronically, socially, fundamentally, television in America is intended and expected to appeal to immense, passive, and heterogeneous audiences.

But mass-audience obsession is not the only characteristic of present-day American TV that renders it ill-suited to the useful communication of serious thought.

(1) Almost anyone, anywhere in the country can receive whatever television offers by a movement of the wrist. So the selective structuring of any audience is chancy and inefficient, far more so than that of a lecture, book, magazine article, or newspaper column.

(2) Television programs, unlike written communication, must be received at a particular time. One's ideal audience may resist this kind of demand, and refuse to respond on call Thursday nights at 9:30. (Future technology may modify this; and, of course, any university lecturer may make the same complaint.)

(3) Television communication must customarily be fit into a very tight time package, usually under (sometimes well under) half an hour. Much can be done in this time by the practiced professional. (Consider Eric Sevareid's astute and efficient use of his two and a half minutes.) But comparisons to serious written communication can seem like studies in frustration. The chapters

of Alistair Cooke's book version of *America* are, on the average, two to three times the length of the television scripts on which they were based. Cooke admitted that he was using the book (in part) to make up for all that he had to leave out on TV.

(4) The very nature of our television receivers and our usual locus of viewing forces a distracted, low-intensity response. This is not a page of clear print to be focused on privately, nor a living stage or commanding screen in a public theatre. It is a small piece of living room (/den/bedroom) furniture. Looking at it, one still sees all the rest of the half-lighted room and takes in yards of peripheral vision. It is generally dull of definition, made up of dots and lines of a mild headachy blur, either bluish-gray or electronic-neon-off-color, utterly unlike print, film, or reality. I believe that the very electron-dot thing that it is (as well as its household furniture role) invites reduced concentration. The sound, typically, is very low fidelity, compared to movies, records, good radio, or life (6000 cycles or less, vs. 20,000 or more), and it too induces a lessened credibility and attention. It is received not in a classroom, study, or communal gathering place, but in one's private lounge. And it is customarily experienced as a domestic social event of the most relaxing, low-energy kind. "Watching television" in this country is what you do *after* the day's work is done, when you haven't the energy to read, or go out—the electronic extension of slippers and pipe. It is something to be chatted over, knitted by, read through, eaten and drunk by. The easy, unthinking, very natural habit of switching back and forth between channels can denature and degrade the autonomous validity of any serious television experience—as can the rhetorical- and reality-status shifts involved in all those "commercial interruptions."

(5) Most people—even one's fellow intellectuals (those who will "have one in the house")—have come to expect television to provide light entertainment, undemanding and passively received. It is what the set is there for, what one turns it on to find. The very nature of most television conditions one's viewing expectations, and makes it difficult (given the thousands of leisure hours they have spent watching commercial network television) for most adult Americans to feel comfortable watching anything as unusual, say, as a typical evening's fare on BBC-2 or the *deuxième chaine* of O.R.T.F.

The viewer comes to expect relatively pallid, sexless, opinionless, lowest-common-denominator material, and to be shocked when he hears or sees things he would take for granted in magazines, newspapers, books, and films. Conversely, he expects the sleekest level of technical finesse—personalities the world recognizes who are utterly in control of the medium; clever escapist and adventure fantasies, if possible featuring these very personalities; the biggest of big-time sport, restructured for his viewing convenience; one-minute packets of illustrated news; the most extravagant care devoted to the production of trifles—and finds it difficult to tolerate the rough amateurishness of anything too "live."

How can the communication of serious thought have any function at all in such a setting, against such expectations?

Even the best, the most serious, the most carefully TV-planned attempts to think before a camera (Kenneth Clark's *Civilisation,* Alistair Cooke's *America,* Jacob Bronowski's *The Ascent of Man,* Russell Connor's *Museum Open House*) have suffered from over-casual, uncritical, even foolish reception on home television receivers. Let me cite one personal example. I watched the *Civilisation* series of thirteen one-hour essays first as full-screen color films in museum theatres, then at home, on television. In the theatre, I found, one concentrated on the *art* and the *ideas.* At home, the nature of the set and the viewing experience emphasized instead the personality of Kenneth Clark, his jokes and clothes, his face and manner, as if he were no more than another $200,000-a-year local news anchorman. (And yet, as one colleague pointed out, at the very least Lord Clark may unconsciously have inculcated an admirable model of Old World civility.) The commanding images of Western art and architecture were (on my old set) reduced and grayed into a twelve-inch travelogue with none of the definition of a good *book,* let alone the persuasive grandeur of the films.

Why, then, would a serious thinker put up with all this inefficiency in order to try to communicate through television? Why abandon the personal control and directness of prose written to be read, the selected, attentive audience of the right magazine, book, or journal? Why, further, put up with all the irrelevant nonsense of the television studio? Endless battles with "visual"-obsessed producers, in mortal terror of your "talking head"; endless quarrels over scripts with people who neither understand nor care for what you're trying to say; orders to cut, orders to simplify; cue cards, blue shirts and face powder; retakes, tedious backchat with trade union yokels. "Try to *smile* a little, Perfesser!" "Slow down, hey!"

Like any professional thinker who has ventured into television, I can tell tales of frustrating, hopelessly non-intellectual arguments over what I could only regard as trivial nonsense. Thousands of precious dollars were spent on a gimmicky, twenty-second opening montage, on an inflatable set that was always leaking. Producers insisted that one film clip was as good as another, and *any* was better than none—even if it was totally irrelevant to what I was saying. What on earth has all this to do with the serious thinker's serious work? Why would he endure it?

Quite possibly, for dubious reasons that have nothing to do with his ideas. For money, perhaps. For fame—there is nothing in the world quite like television fame. People will come to know him, personally, thousands of them—even in a 1.0 rated show. The showman in him may be gratified, the desire to show off, to display face and voice. He may feel anxious to "participate" more visibly in his own time, make himself and his ideas more accessible, and escape the uncertain self-image of the reclusive intellectual. He will be stopped by strangers, receive far more letters than any book or article would ever attract. He may find that this new kind of notoriety—popular, visible, *TV Guide* fame—leads to other invitations, enabling him to continue and enlarge it: the lecture circuit, talk shows, invitations to "host" *new* television series, invitations to write (more likely edit) mass editions of popular books—all this to capitalize on his television fame.

Yet desire for fame is, of itself, nothing to be ashamed of. It need not make a person any less an intellectual, any more than it makes Julia Child any less a good chef (or at least a good cooking teacher). But the television situation does probably limit the field to a particular *kind* of intellectual: one who is glib and non-reclusive, one who *is* to some degree a showman and a ham; one who is, for whatever occult reasons, "telegenic"; one who does, in fact, crave a degree of popular fame beyond that attainable by the print intellectual.

This may all be rationalized, or even seriously understructured, by a missionary impulse: an urgent desire to reach the masses, to communicate serious ideas or higher culture to the People—to educate the electorate to more responsible citizenship; to inform Americans about the truth of their past; to ward off barbarism; to develop a taste for Finer Things; to offer higher education to the millions of men and women who will never get to a college or university.

In television situations the intellectual may find that the percentage of his audience paying attention to what he says runs in inverse order to audience size. The small numbers of people (by television standards) who choose to watch *Sunrise Semester* classes, or serious intellectual series virtually devoid of "production values" (Crane Brinton's or Abraham Sachar's history lectures, for example), probably do care enough to attend closely to what is being said. Better visuals, the use of music, more stylish narrators and narration—all that media professionals think of as "television"—may attract much larger audiences for the Clarks and Cookes, but

(a) the "production values"—the TVness of TV—may themselves distract from the efficient communication of serious ideas;

(b) a large fraction of the audience attracted by the production values may well be interested only, or primarily, in such peripheral treats; and

(c) the writers' ideas may have had to be more drastically simplified (adapted both to the "visuals" and to the larger audience) than those of the less popular, straightforward TV lecturers.

My own experience as a thinker on TV may or may not be representative. I find that I do prepare scripts in a studied, rhetorical-for-TV way, with colloquial asides, a conversational flow, repetitions for assistance and effect, and so on. I many times yield to a temptation to gratuitous wit, which viewers love; phrase-make more than I ever would in print or the lecture hall; sometimes pretend to an unfelt ardor or anger for the sake of drama; and sacrifice key ideas or examples because my producer can't illustrate them. I try to keep discussions linear rather than harmonic or complex, so that each segment in time is clear and complete by itself. I tend to avoid the abstract, constantly make reference to real-world analogies and situations, and pretend to test or challenge my own thinking by imagining and incorporating the viewer's own reactions.

These may be tendencies which fit a particular kind of thinker for television, or they may be bad habits that television creates. In my relatively free choice of subjects and approaches, I (and my producers) have tended to favor the readily illustratable, so that literature (for example) has been given less than its due in my coverage of the arts.

But all this, so far, is only one side of the story.

The attentive, fertile fraction of a typical television audience may be smaller than that of a university lecture or serious article. But the total number attending may be so much larger that even this small fraction may turn out to be the greatest serious audience the thinker has ever attracted. Crane Brinton's "rating" may have been near to invisible, but surely his total television audience each week would have filled his Harvard lecture hall many times over. And although what I have called the "TVness of TV" may attract the "wrong" audience and distract from serious thought, there *are* occasions when it can support and enrich intellectual communication.

It is not easy to determine what kinds of serious thinking television can serve best. I tend to believe that abstract ideas—ideas that are neither reducible to documentary presentation, nor fundamentally hortatory/argumentative—do not lend themselves well to television presentation. But the first person to find a good visual or dramatic equivalent for traditional printed forms of abstract thought (philosophy, linguistics, mathematics, many forms of science and social science) will prove me wrong, and I hope someone can. Although their efforts have so far proved unproductive, the BBC has spent two years and ₤200,000 trying to contrive a series on economics, of all things (starring John Kenneth Galbraith), that would have at least the same potency and vitality as Kenneth Clark's series on Western art. *Sesame Street* and *The Electric Company*, a few extraordinary documentaries, and certain British science and children's programs have changed many of my ideas about what television can and cannot communicate.

But my suspicion is that television can add very little to many kinds of serious speculation. Even a "talking head," it seems to me, can only distract from the pure space one needs around certain ideas. (Shut up, head; go away and let me think.) Television precludes one's following thought processes at one's own proper pace, circling round a sequence, moving forward and back to compare this idea with that, to verify and test; it disallows much in the way of essential, internal "talking back." And one *must* be allowed these freedoms, I believe, this ability to participate and respond, for abstract, non-narrative intellectual communication to take place. This may be the archaic bias of one educated through the privacy of print; but I think that certain forms of intellectual communication demand a kind of mental space, a room to move and respond that television as we know it cannot permit.

The apparently personal and dramatic nature of what one sees on the television screen renders the medium especially apt for the thinker who wants to argue a point, to *convince* his auditors, like the best trial lawyers, critics, lecturers (and, I suppose, advertisers and politicians). Not all intellectuals are of this sort, and not all ideas bear a dynamic, rhetorical component.

The mere "talking head" is scorned by many television professionals. Some of them regard the dour face of a person thinking out loud as simply "not television" and would a hundred times rather substitute or cut to more vivid and varied forms of imagery. But a talking head can still be wondrously dramatic, even hypnotic—and precisely *in* its ability to argue and convince. There remains an extraordinary potential for drama in the combined voice, eyes, and living presence of someone thinking aloud, as certain experiments in news reporting and discussion by actual reporters (like KQED—San Francisco's *Newsroom*) have made clear. There are times when a face alone on the screen, declaring, debating, exhorting, may still be the most powerful and effective image television can present. To dramatize ideas by getting excited about them, to look the viewer "straight in the eye" (i.e., the camera lens) and win his concern or assent by the appearance of sincerity, to obtain awe with a whisper, to *convince* that mass of invisible strangers that you care and that they should care too—for the telegenic thinker with a mission, the "real presence" factor of television is invaluable.

The two most successful TV thinkers so far have both been thinkers with a mission. Alistair Cooke was seriously troubled by the fact that most Americans knew so little of their own history. Kenneth Clark was deeply worried about what he thought of as "civilization," about the loss of fundamental values in modern times. Both men were acting under moralistic impulses, both chose as their subjects the things they cared about most, and both took to TV in order to make use of its great persuasive powers.

They were also interested, of course, in all that its sophisticated arsenal of audio-visual techniques could bring to aid them in their mission. Television can do *so much more* than transmit the monodrama of even the liveliest, most histrionic Talking Head. And it would be foolish of the missionary-intellectual interested in its audience not to make use of its remarkable powers.

Art history or criticism (Lord Clark's field) can be admirably served by television, particularly if the art historian or critic is able to collaborate knowingly and sympathetically with his photographers, researchers, and editors to bring the television image into coincidence with his thought. So too with scholarship or criticism of dance, film, theatre, opera, television itself; in every case where the subject is itself a *thing seen,* the commentator-specialist would be foolish to ignore television's illustrative powers. I can imagine, for example, a whole series of priceless television explorations of the theory, history, and art of film—*and* of television—once problems of re-broadcast rights and archival research could be resolved. No other medium could do the job better.

As we move away from fields where the very subject is visible and televisable, we must take care that the production elements—the TV "visuals"— do in fact support rather than blur or distort our case. *History* can be well served, because the past has left so many visible images of itself, both in surviving places and things, and in paintings, prints, and photographs. Recent history is especially suited to analysis on television, as witness all the successful *World at War* and *Twentieth Century* series, whose producers were able to draw on such immense newsreel collections. Certain forms of *science,* especially natural science (zoology, entomology, botany, to a lesser degree geology and astronomy) deal with visible and sometimes marvelously telegenic subjects, and have long been a staple of TV. Other sciences, farther removed from the photographable object (the health sciences, for example), can still be rendered dramatically and cogently visible. *Political science* and *anthropology* could, I think, be substantially aided by television's visual powers; but here one's choices would have to be very scrupulously made. It would be very easy for the imagery to vulgarize to such an extent that one's point would be lost, or even to work against one's essential ideas.

But each specialist—providing he is familiar with television, knows what it requires and how it works—may be able to conceive ways in which the communication of his ideas can be strengthened, rather than cheapened or distorted, by proper collaboration with the television professional.

In time, I believe, a new kind of expert will emerge, one who naturally, almost automatically, thinks in both terms at once: a person who works out his own unique, front line ideas, and *at the same time* conceives of a means of communicating them over TV. He will be as trained, alert, and sensitive in his visual imagination, his concern for optimum communication, as he is in his own special field. Michael Arlen once speculated what would happen to the nightly news from Vietnam if someone risked sending over a Godard or Antonioni to film it—that is, a master of *visual* thinking, not a print journalist translated to TV. David Attenborough, who alternates between directing all BBC-TV programming and trekking off to remote jungles to make his own natural science documentaries, strikes me as a possible model of the New Man I have in mind.

At the moment it's not a very common type. Our educational system demands years of dedicated effort in order for one to become an expert *either* in the ways and means of television *or* in literary criticism, bacteriology, or any other specialized field. Today the intellectuals who are willing to make use of television are often those who have given up (or never aspired to) primary work of their own, those who have accepted the careers of retailers, rather than manufacturers of ideas: teachers, critics, professional popularizers, and journalists, rather than scientists, artists, researchers, or historians.

Clark and Cooke—to return to the two most successful models at hand—fall somewhere between the original thinker and the retail popularizer. Both, as I noted, are men of a histrionic bent and a missionary temper. And both were made watchable and successful, were "turned into television," by *television professionals*, notably by their common producer, Michael Gill of BBC-TV, who was clearly as vital a contributor as either of the two thinker-performers with whom he has so intimately and fruitfully worked. ("The extent to which Clark drew upon Gill, and Gill drew upon Clark, is not open to measurement or even speculation ... Kenneth Clark and Michael Gill constituted a successful collaboration as did Mozart and Da Ponte, or Gilbert with Sullivan," according to Huw Wheldon, Managing Director of BBC television.)

In this "meeting of equals," it is usually the television producer who is obliged to be the more patient, the more generous, the more diplomatic—if only because of the traditional public prestige of the print-intellectual, and the fact that the latter is now the visible "star." But it is only through this kind of enlightened collaboration that serious ideas can be, finally, turned into television, and served as well as the medium can serve them.

And yet everything I've suggested so far may be too timid, too dependent on pre-television modes of thought. Lectures in colorful and appropriate settings, or intercut with tactful illustrations, are still lectures, one might claim, and not television—or at least not television used to its fullest potential.

One of the problems of such discussions is what might be called "The Watershed of 1950"—to assign a date to the beginning of the American television age. The intellectual born and educated before 1950 may spend much of his life trying to wish television away, or at least to convert it into something closer to his own past of reading, reason, naive wonder, and private imagination. A roomful of humanists in Palo Alto last year agreed that BBC's *War and Peace* was *their* idea of "good television." What they really meant, I think, was that it was an acceptable part of their own literary past, tastefully rendered into this dubious new form.

Like them, I have a vested interest in print. I might put down a book (even *War and Peace*) to watch *War and Peace;* but not to watch *Mission: Impossible.* I can't escape my own television-less past. But younger men and women, the generation after 1950, will think about television in entirely different ways. They will accept its pervasiveness, its slickness and tricks, its limitations and potentials far more freely and guiltlessly than I can. For them, if television renders school more boring, reading more difficult, and prolonged close concentration near to impossible, well *so be it*; so much the worse for schools, reading, and concentration. While I dream of long sabbaticals with bags full of books on some television-free island, they are back home in the studios and schools thinking up solutions to all the communications problems I've described—and in *television's own terms.*

It is difficult for one unpossessed of a native video sensibility, one for whom TV *is* a second language, to conceive of what the possibilities might be. But experiments like *Sesame Street, Laugh-In, TW3,* and *Monty Python's Flying Circus* may help open eyes and imaginations—as may some of the advanced cathode-ray tube experimentation of television artists, and the fresh approaches to news and documentaries of radical production communes like TVTV and Video Free America. Comedy stars may front serio-comic presentations of critical issues. Current events may be presented not as news, but in dramatized or satiric form, thus capitalizing on the public's supposed inability to distinguish hard news on the tube from entertainment drama. One can conceive of a dramatic series that deals not with a sentimentalized, nostalgic view of poverty past, but with *real* poverty today. *Cinema verité,* in the right hands (like Frederick Wiseman's), and thoughtfully edited, may offer far more than the exhibitionism and voyeurism of *An American Family* and its followers. The adult sophistication of Czech and Polish cartoons might one day find a regular place on American TV screens.

But these are only random speculations. The possibilities are endless. What is really needed is some way of *ending,* or at least meliorating the situation described in the first part of this paper, whereby many of the best, potentially most useful minds in America refuse to have anything to do with television.

I have already suggested some good reasons for their refusal. There are others. Most American intellectuals are in the employ of colleges and universities, many of which traditionally do not admire or reward "thinking on television." The derision of one's print-oriented colleagues, the very practical matter of raises and promotions, may keep many American professors committed to communicating by the article and the book. So may the dismay of hearing one's prize thoughts lost forever in the night air as soon as uttered.

"How do you keep a first-rate mind in a third-rate industry?" asked David Webster of the BBC. And yet, surprisingly to many Americans, British television has long done precisely that. It came as a shock to me to learn that the great linguistic philosopher A. J. Ayer was a well-known television personality in Britain, and that Asa Briggs—whom I had known only as a distinguished social historian—once hired a brass band for his Leeds radio program and personally participated in *TW3!*

On this side of the Atlantic, Edmund Wilson sent out printed "Mr. Wilson does not" postcards refusing *any* invitation to appear on radio or television. Instead of a Wilson, or one of Britain's professionally and popularly respected telly-dons, we were left with the likes of Clifton Fadiman. *The New Yorker* has Pauline Kael, NBC Gene Shalit. Third-rate minds in a third-rate industry.

That this is so is perhaps lamentable, but, as I point out, perfectly understandable. For many reasons, the scrupulous thinking man may not *wish* to identify himself with anything so vulgar and debased as American television, and it may well not be in his professional interest to do so.

And yet television is there; it is now the dominant mode of communication in this country; it is not going to go away. The intellectual community continues to ignore it, I believe, at great disservice to itself. "Most people get direction from electronic media and not from books," Peter Wood has said. "So eventually, television as a visual medium will *have* to be used by intellectuals and humanists."

Good things *do* happen on television, because good men do get into TV and learn to live with it. They accept the perpetual state of war with "Them," the vulgarizers and market researchers and network executives—at PBS as at CBS. Oh, they compromise, of course, far more than they may ever have had to do at the academy—in order to reach the hundred thousand, the million, the ten million people. ("Through compromise to integrity" was the not entirely facetious private motto of DuPont's prizewinning *Show of the Month.*) They learn how much they can do in thirty minutes—or in ninety seconds. They learn to shut up, to collaborate, to angle for good adjacencies, to think visually themselves.

A few pages ago I complained of all the degrading, anti-intellectual stunts I have had to put up with in order to make use of TV. And yet I *do* make use of it, and intend to go on doing so. I've come to accept the colored shirts, the long waits, the standups and repeats (each time with undiminished speed and enthusiasm), the fact that viewers remember facial tics much more vividly than original ideas. I've tried to develop not only patience with, but also the ability to *collaborate* with the "TV-ness of TV," and to stop marching into the studio all impatient and huffy, demanding the right to lecture uninterrupted: "After all, it is *my* show!"

No, it's not. It's the producer's, fundamentally. You, Mr. Thinker (A. J. Ayer, Stanley Kauffmann, whoever you are), are what behind-the-camera types designate as "The Talent": the feed, the outsider. You're *not* television—until they turn you into it.

I knew I had passed a certain threshold when I began to conceive a proposed television series on architectural preservation in terms of visual sequences, even visual *gimmicks*, instead of flawless linear chains of eloquent discourse: old prints dissolving into photographs, fine old buildings destroyed (and then magically rebuilt) by films shown first in slow motion and then in reverse.

The secret is not to ignore or despise the audience-trapping tricks of *Hogan's Heroes* or *The Dating Game,* but to use them *better,* and to better purpose. If successful and only moderately unscrupulous politicians can learn to manipulate television in their own interests, surely the wisest men and women in America can learn to do so too, in pursuit of more noble and more unselfish goals.

It will, as Peter Wood says, *have* to happen, or else American universities will begin to assume the reactionary and isolated status of monasteries after the Reformation. Their pre-1950 faculties will be talking more and more to an alien breed of student. Already, news programs make use of economists, moon-watches of space scientists, documentaries of behind-the-scenes specialists who provide ideas and check accuracy. One day these economists and space scientists and specialists may well learn enough to be running their own shows.

I am not very adept at future-speculation. But it is possible to imagine that the years to come may bring variations in television technology that *do* permit the viewer to "make spaces" and talk back, to collaborate more actively with the transmitter, to pace and structure the information flow according to his own needs, as one does today in language labs and with other self-teaching machines.

Some such radical innovation is probably essential if television is to be used efficiently for the transmission of serious thought. As it is, the enforced passivity and low-intensity response of almost all American television probably do "soften" brains rather than stimulate them and serve an almost Huxleyan tranquillizing function. Television—one of the most successful products of a technological age—is called upon more and more to function as the painkiller, illusion-maker, and reality substitute for the disoriented citizens of that age. Where in fact their world is messy, unfair, technologically run, out of their grasp, and devoid of much human community, television fosters the illusions of democratic participation, awareness and understanding, order and control, the full and rational presentation and discussion of problems, of human contact and conversation—even, on occasion, of deep thought and cultural sophistication.

The very lavish totality of its illusion-making has made alternatives to television seem increasingly inadequate: magicians are less magic, the circus is not so gaudy, going out is too much trouble, the theatre too demanding, live sport harder to watch, real controversy too painful. Each year, the university teacher is obliged to presume in his typical student a lessened attention span and ability to read whole books.

I believe (I do not know) that present forms of television, and present habits of receiving it, reduce one's ability to make his own world: to judge, select, and participate. I believe (I do not know) that they reduce one's tolerance to stillness and silence, to mental space and irresolution. By increasing one's tolerance to noise, chopped variety, imagistic chaos, and the atomization of time, they may shrivel up patience and tolerance generally—tolerance of a thousand and one "real world" situations: overlong meetings, amateur entertainment, unfamous people, ineloquent politicians, unsmooth conversation, scoreless ties in sport—without instituting in the viewer the least urge or impulse to correct an uncomfortable situation. He can always stay home and change the channel.

TV has *become* reality for many people, because it is more tolerable than any other. "Real" reality is too impossibly complex to deal with. Television, which has helped to make both real reality and our perception of it so painful (by exaggerating our needs, by displaying to us more of the world's treasures and evils than we can cope with), provides answers and palliatives. Television we can bear.

Until all this changes radically, there is probably not much hope for more than occasional, at best weakly effective, injections of "serious thought" into television programming. The very situation is too false, too dependent on illusion, for serious ideas to feel at home. Only when some form of feedback, of *response* by the viewer, some built-in circuit of self-criticism is added can television begin to be a congenial home for open intellectual activity.

There is yet another possibility: that a future out of my imaginative reach may be able to contrive *visual* equivalents for ideas I can conceive of only in words. Television itself may be developing new forms of cognition by *means* of its own symbols, which will enable generations formed under its watchful eye to deal with difficult concepts entirely in its language. Then again, they may be able to dispense with many of the agonizing intellectual problems for which words seem essential.

But there my own head stops.

P.S. I realize there is something self-contradictory, not to say schizophrenic in this paper, which on the one hand details the hopeless unfitness of American television for the work of serious thinkers, and on the other begs the serious thinker to make greater use of it. But the contradiction exists in my own mind as well, and it would be deceptive to try to edit it out here.

D . L .

Footnotes

1.   *What began as a collection of more or less private speculations has been expanded and enriched by the thinking of several of my co-participants at the Aspen, Colorado, Conference on "Television as a Social and Cultural Force" in August 1974. They may well recognize here their unacknowledged ideas.*

2.   *Milton Berle, way back then, managed an unthinkable 75%. Block-buster Hollywood films (The Birds, The Godfather, Bridge on the River Kwai), and "Charlie Brown's Christmas Show" regularly seize 40-50% or more.*

In all communication, whether by words or by images, there is always some editorializing. There is always a subjective aspect because we are what we are, human beings, each with our own set of experiences, our own set of prejudices. Now the curious thing is that in communicating by words, editorializing can be much more easily detected because we are very familiar with words and the methods of using words. . . . The image always has a point of view, but it's more insidious. Sometimes we don't realize there is a point of view. There is no such thing as a perfect photograph that gives us a perfect image. The photographer, knowingly or unknowingly, always chooses a certain aspect of the subject, and that is a form of editorializing. Sometimes it's very innocent, sometimes very dangerous, because we have such a naive idea about the truthfulness of an image as against a distrust of verbal description or argument.

Julius Bloom

Newspaper News and Television News

Paul H. Weaver

The American newspaper as we know it today has been an established and essentially unchanging institution for upwards of 70 years. The same can hardly be said of television. As recently as 30 years ago it was nothing but a gleam in the entrepreneurial eye, and over the intervening decades it has passed fitfully through its infancy and adolescence. Today, however, television can fairly be said to have attained its majority and entered adulthood. Fully mature it obviously isn't, but adult it most certainly is; what was once a congeries of open-ended possibilities is now a settled and distinctive reality.

The fact that television is now a full-fledged institution and mode of communication implies, among other things, that it has finally become a fit subject for serious scholarship. For the humanist, television provides a settled *genre*, or family of *genres,* for study and criticism. These may not be high forms, but they are forms nevertheless and as such are presumably worthy of attention. For the social scientist, the institution of television itself, and its impact on other institutions and social processes, is at last something that can be looked at without fear that tomorrow everything will suddenly be different. And for everyone's scrutiny there is the central reality of television as a settled and powerful force in American civilization, actively at work affecting our culture, politics, economy, and individual lives.

What difference has the advent of television made to American society? Nobody really knows, of course; it is still too early to tell, and until recently critics and scholars have generally dismissed TV out of hand, calling it "chewing gum for the eyes" or some other expression of thoughtless contempt.

Paul Weaver is Associate Editor of *Fortune* Magazine, and was formerly Assistant Professor of Government at Harvard. He has written extensively on journalism and the role of the press.

In these pages I would nevertheless like to offer a few tentative thoughts about the nature, assumptions, and political consequences of one element of modern television, the nightly network news program. It is clear to me that, in comparison to newspaper news, television news is not just "more of the same." Despite their many shared characteristics, newspapers and television differ in several fundamental respects and consequently tend to shape public perceptions and opinions in different ways.

I.

It is more or less impossible to think coherently about the comparison between newspaper news and television news until one grasps a simple but all-important truth: that news is a *genre*, a distinctive mode of writing and of depicting experience, and that any comparisons between newspapers and television must at least begin by analyzing the variant of this *genre* that each represents. Economic, technological, legal, and social considerations may be explored later, but to begin with what one is talking about are two related but not identical modes of expression and vision. And since expression and vision are so heavily influenced by culture, one cannot for the most part think coherently about such modes in the abstract—one must look at journalism *in a given place* and *at a stated time*. National and historical differences within journalism are extremely large. In what follows, I shall be concerned solely with American newspapers and American TV as they exist today.

In order to discourage anyone from entertaining an exaggerated notion of how different these two media are, and with the hope of putting their real differences in some perspective, let me begin by sketching what seem to me to be their most important common characteristics. Many of the vices and virtues that people attribute to television or newspapers are in fact not unique to the medium in question but are instead characteristics of news as such.

First, newspaper news and television news are alike in being varieties of journalism, which means that both consist of a current account of current events. ("Criticism of the moment at the moment," was James's useful formulation.) This two-fold contemporaneity—the present as a subject matter, and the present as the perspective in time from which it is described—is what accounts for the intense and universal appeal of journalism, and also for the extraordinary difficulty journalism encounters in achieving a depiction of events which experience and criticism affirm to be coherent, balanced, and reliable. This difficulty, it should be emphasized, is an inherent one for which there can be no solution; the best one can hope for is a recognition of the difficulty, an earnest effort to cope with it, and a general scaling down of claims and expectations all around. However that may be, television and newspapers share the appeal and the difficulty of contemporaneity more or less equally. The familiar criticism that TV is under greater time pressure, and therefore is less thoughtful, is essentially false. The criticism applies to both media.

Second, newspaper news and television news are alike in "covering" current events by means of reportage, i.e., factual description of what an on-the-scene observer of the event in question saw and heard. Thus news in America has long possessed all the distinctive advantages of reportage—concreteness, immediacy, and faithfulness to the particularity of events. But by the same token it has also been prone to the special weaknesses of reportage, chief of which are a relative inability to depict complexity and ambiguity and a powerful disinclination to pursue the meta-observational questions which illuminate complexity and ambiguity. A further shortcoming of reportage is that it increases the likelihood that the newsman, in the course of gathering information about a given event by being on the scene, will alter the event. This "Heisenberg effect" is an everyday occurrence in modern journalism and can be seen in the omnipresence of "pseudo-events" (happenings engineered by sources for the purpose of being reported), in the common practice of "milking the news," and in the much rarer instances of deliberate "staging" of events by newsmen desperate for a good story to report. Newspapers and TV are equally prone to these pathologies.

Third, newspaper news and television news are alike in being accounts of events that are vocationally-produced by special-purpose organizations. News is gathered and written by persons whose full-time occupation is to gather and write news. Thus newsmen may be said to be specialists—members of a distinct occupational community that has its distinctive traditions, concerns, and ways of doing things. Inevitably, news reflects the specialized ethos of the journalistic community and is shaped by its structure and processes, even though the intention of news is to speak to, and embody, the general concerns of the average citizen.

Fourth, newspaper and television news are alike in being essentially melodramatic accounts of current events. Partly by virtue of their focus on "events" and partly as a result of the traditions which define the ethos of the newsman and the structure of the news story, both newspapers and television depict events as actions that carry forward an implicit and usually extremely simplistic line of dramatic action. Thus events derive their journalistic identity in no small measure from the dramatistic fictions which newsmen and sources spin around them. One consequence of this practice is that news has historically defined the present as a period of transition—as an outgrowth of the past and a prefiguration of the future, yet different from both; as a time of discontinuity rather than continuity, of instability rather than stability, and of danger, crisis, struggle, and adventure rather than the reverse. Another consequence is the way in which the decisions of news organizations about the newsworthiness of a particular event quickly come to be self-fulfilling prophecies: what one prints today establishes a line of action which identifies related events tomorrow as being newsworthy, the printing of which both confirms the validity of the first day's decision and points to events still farther in the future as being worthy of coverage. So faddism and sensationalism are tendencies of both media.

Finally, newspaper news and television news in America are alike in using the same themes, formulas, and symbols in constructing the lines of melodramatic action which give meaning and identity to events. The two media, in other words, are cut from the same intellectual and rhetorical cloth. For instance, both newspapers and television typically report events associated with political campaigns in terms of a generalized image of politics as a horse race. Events associated with major changes in public policy, by contrast, are generally presented in terms of a model of policy-making as the undertaking of expert and well-intentioned leaders acting in the public interest. The failure of policy is ordinarily described according to a scenario in which existing policies are defended by officials and other interested parties for selfish motives against the opposition of an aroused public opinion indignantly demanding reform. These generalized images are but a few of the many formulas that give concrete expression to the two central themes that run, colliding with each other as they do so, throughout all newspaper and television journalism in America—the populist notion that the people should rule directly in their own felt interests, and the republican notion that established institutions should rule in behalf of the public interest under the scrutiny of the electorate.

II.

So much for similarities; now for some of the differences which make the advent of television journalism an event of no small moment in America political history. Undoubtedly, the most obvious of these differences is a structural one. In comparison to newspaper news, television news is far more coherently organized and tightly unified, and this is true of the individual TV and newspaper news story as well as of the TV and newspaper news aggregate as a whole (the newspaper edition and the TV news program). This difference is associated with the fact that TV is organized and presented in time, whereas the newspaper edition is organized only in space.

The difference in structure becomes most apparent when one considers newspaper editions and TV news programs as wholes. Though both are limited in volume, the newspaper contains a vastly larger number of stories by a factor of something on the order of ten. This occurs because the newspaper, being organized in space, can feasibly publish many more stories, and much more text, than most readers care to read; its contents are thus an *à la carte* menu which the reader rapidly scans and from which he selects a "meal" according to his interests and time. Inevitably, therefore, the contents of the typical newspaper edition are chosen to be extremely diverse—are chosen, in fact, *not* to be read in their entirety by a single reader. There is, in consequence, a loose, open-ended, discursive quality to the contents and structure of the newspaper edition.

It is precisely the reverse with the television news program. Being organized in time, it cannot so easily present news *a la carte*: to "scan" all the possible stories, the viewer would have to see all of them in their entirety in the first place before choosing which ones to view—which is an absurdity. The television news program is thus a *table d'hôte*, a collection of stories selected and arranged to be seen in their entirety by every viewer without reducing the size or interest of the audience as the program proceeds. The consequence is that the television news program contains many fewer stories and that the ones it does contain are chosen carefully for their interest and balance and are presented as a relatively coherent and integrated package.

Thus, whereas the contents of the newspaper make up a diverse, numerous, often inchoate aggregate, the elements of the television news program typically form a unified whole. They seldom if ever attain perfect unity, of course; the materials of the real world, though malleable in television journalism, are not *that* malleable. But almost invariably there are several stories in a given program that exhibit a common theme or mood, and frequently there are further stories designed to provide contrast, emphasis, or development. This does not happen by accident; it is intentional on the part of TV newsmen, and the fact that it is intentional is proof that the underlying goal of the television news program is to attain the condition of wholeness, to exhibit theme, structure, and unity.

One consequence of this is that the TV news program tends to present a single, unified interpretation of the day's events *as a whole* and to construe periods of time as having a single defining movement, action, or mood. To the extent that we think or speak of the day's events holistically as good, bad, hopeful, discouraging, dramatic, boring, or whatever—and of course we all do this constantly—we are thinking in the mode of television journalism. In newspapers, by contrast, the events of the day rarely have anywhere near so clear a thematic identity; the newspaper's day is always a comparative mishmash.

Though it is not widely recognized and is often actually denied, precisely the same general relationship exists between the television news story and the newspaper news story. We are used to thinking of the TV news story as a slight, weak, and unsophisticated expository instrument in comparison to the newspaper news story. TV, according to conventional wisdom, is essentially a "headline service" that must content itself with formulaic capsule summaries of the top "spot news" stories of the day; newspapers, by contrast, have the time, space, and capacity to produce long, meaty, analytic, more fully-realized accounts of what's going on. Yet the reality is exactly the reverse, as a glance at the scripts of just a few film news stories immediately demonstrates. Allowing for the fact that the newspaper news story *is* longer and does contain more raw data, the truth is that ordinarily it is the television news story which is more analytical, which more consistently and insistently goes beneath and beyond the surface of events to exhibit the larger trends and meanings of current affairs, which achieves the more integrated and coherent exposition of the reporter's findings, and which constitutes the more flexible and sophisticated reportorial instrumentality.

The standard newspaper news story is organized according to the principle of the "inverted pyramid."[1] Its subject and focus is a single, unitary event as defined in one or two sentences (the headline and lead paragraph). Having stated in the simplest and most reductionist of terms the bare bones of the event (who, what, where, when, and so on), the newspaper news story—*every* newspaper news story—has already achieved a kind of completeness and can be terminated at that point without rendering it unintelligible; if it is published in this form we call it an "item" or "filler." (A significant proportion of the "filler items" published by our newspapers, interestingly enough, are in fact major stories from out-of-town and foreign newspapers which have been cut off after the second or third paragraph in precisely this way.) But the news story need not be, and characteristically is not, terminated at this point. Instead it goes on, in a quasi-random sequence of syntactically crude sentences and disjointed paragraphs, to adduce additional data that elaborate on this or that aspect of the story-, topic-, and event-defining headline and lead. In theory, these data are to be presented in descending order of importance, and to some extent they are—the objective here being to enable an editor to cut as much material as needs to be cut to make the story fit the available space in the shortest possible time while doing the least substantive damage (he cuts the material at the end of the story), and to maximize the ease with which a reader can decide he has read as much of the story as suits his purposes (he reads down the story until he has had enough). But for the most part the data are presented in a quasi-random order, for the simple reason that they are all roughly co-equal in importance—or rather in unimportance, since the fact remains that the story stands on its own with all but the first few paragraphs eliminated.

The television news story is radically different.[2] Unlike the newspaper news story, which is designed *not* to be read in its entirety while still achieving intelligibility, the television news story is a whole that is designed to be fully intelligible only when viewed in its entirety. Its focus is therefore upon a theme which runs throughout the story and which develops as the story moves from its beginning to its middle and then to its end. Information, narrative, sound, and pictures are selected and organized to illustrate the theme and to provide the necessary development.

Events in the newspaper sense of happenings that can be defined and comprehended in a single sentence are but the occasion of the television news story, not its *raison d'être*. In fact, a surprisingly large proportion of TV news stories are not about events in any intelligible sense and do not pretend to be;

and of those that do deal with events nearly all either dramatize or re-enact them, or treat them as incidental epiphenomena of the larger phenomena or ideas which are the true thematic focus. But whatever the case, the TV news story, structurally, is virtually incapable of limiting itself to the simple event-naming and embroidering function performed by the newspaper news story; inevitably it goes into, beneath, or beyond the ostensive event to fix upon something else—a process, mood, trend, condition, irony, relationship, or whatever else seems a suitable theme in the circumstances.

A number of conclusions follow from the structural differences between newspaper and television news. One, clearly, is that television news is a far more flexible and intellectually accommodating form than the newspaper variety: more "interpretive," less constrained by the daily flow of events, and less committed to the newspaper's narrow, one-day-only perspective in time. (Whether TV makes proper use of this ability, or squanders it, is another question, on which more later.) Second, it seems equally clear that, as regards the interpretation of current events, television is capable of being—and ordinarily is—far more monolithic than the newspaper. Just as a single idea or theme governs the selection and presentation of all the information in the TV news story to a far greater extent than in the looser, more discursive, less "disciplined" newspaper story, so can a single theme or mood come to determine the contents of an entire TV news program and thus minutely shape its depiction of current affairs as a whole—something that is essentially impossible in a newspaper edition. Finally, and in consequence, the structure of TV news renders its contents far more completely within the practical, day-to-day, discretionary control of the TV news executive than is the case with newspapers, the content of which is by comparison more powerfully influenced by events, sources, and other external or uncontrollable forces.

III.

A second major difference between the two media is associated with the fact that television is both visual and aural, while the newspaper is visual only. It thus becomes possible—and television, from the beginning, has chosen to exploit this possibility—for TV news to rely on spoken narrative as against the written narrative of the newspaper. This in itself is a substantial difference, but its consequences are made all the more powerful by the distinctive ways in which the two media have chosen to execute their narrative functions.

Newspaper news adopts an intensely impersonal narrative voice. In part, this means that the reporter, in writing his story, never speaks in the first person, but the matter goes far beyond that. The reporter also never makes reference to his own actions in observing events and finding facts; there is never any explicit allusion to the reporter's own awareness of the motives of sources, the probable validity of quoted statements, the extent to which the story at hand confirms or falsifies previous stories, and so forth. Moreover, the news story is couched in the extremely narrow and stylized vocabulary which has become standard for all modern news writing; it too helps to expunge any intimation of the reporter's identity and consciousness. The almost random structure of the newspaper news story and the crude syntax of the prose have much the same effect, making it nearly impossible for the reporter to express his best personal understanding of the subject at hand and of the relationships and contexts of the data he adduces. In short, the form of the newspaper news story systematically obscures any trace of the actual person who is doing the writing, who has observed the event in question at first hand, and who presumably has developed a critical understanding of it. What remains in the story is only a residue of impersonal statements of unambiguously observable fact; the newspaper news story narrates the flow of current events in the rigorous and remote voice of the scientific paper.

This impersonal narrator endows newspaper journalism with a number of advantages and disadvantages. As for the advantages, there is first the fact that the newspaper's style tends to maximize the reader's belief in the truthfulness and dispassion of what the newspaper prints. It is a style which suggests an author who is so passionately scrupulous about facts that he will write literally nothing that an independent investigator could not verify as a fact. It suggests an author so rigorous in his positivism that he will not even imply relationships or nuances. And it suggests as well an author who is so dedicated to the ideal of objective neutrality in all things that he will make literally no reference, however modest or oblique, to his own person. The voice of the newspaper, in short, suggests an author who is a fact-machine, and nothing more.

Or rather almost nothing more: for the reality, of course, is that behind every newspaper news story there lurks a real, flesh-and-blood author who, being only human, does have real thoughts, real personal experience and knowledge, and real feelings. The disjointed, low-key, facts-only, simple-declar-ative-sentence prose this real person writes powerfully suggests a kind of deliberate repression of self and thus establishes within newspaper writing a distinct intensity, an undercurrent of taut emotion in the manner of Heming-way. Thus to the quasi-scientific authority of the fact-machine there is added the interest and drama inherent in the intensity radiated by this deliberately impersonal person.

There are also some disadvantages, however. The newspaper's laconic, facts-only voice prevents the reporter from conveying to the reader the substantial proportion of his knowledge and feel for the event at hand that cannot be formulated as statements of unambiguously observable fact. As a result, this information is simply denied to the reader. Moreover, interrelation-ships among the facts presented in the news story are rendered deeply ambiguous by the disjointedness of their exposition. The narrowness of the news story's vocabulary also obliterates complexity and nuance; events are effectively reduced to things that are fully described by their overt physical attributes and their legal-bureaucratic status. In the last analysis, then, this is a voice that does almost as much to make it hard for the reader to understand events as it does to help him—and this in turn calls into question the intentions of the real author, the reporter. What kind of person would present himself as a fact-machine—as a person who is not human and who exercises no judgment? What sort of person sometimes tells the reader less than he has reason to believe? Who would write things whose implication he knows to be false or misleading? The answer is easy: someone who at best is gravely confused and at worst is utterly dishonest with himself and his reader. He is a person who refuses to assume responsibility for the meaning of what he writes; who evades the obligations that are instantly created between author and reader the minute one sets pen to paper; and who cynically manipulates the reader's trust. The author of the news story, in sum, seems to want to bamboozle the reader as much as to inform him, and in this sense he is an unreliable narrator.

The narrative style of television news is the polar opposite of that embodied in the conventions of newspaper writing. It is, above all, a *personal* voice that tells the day's news on the tube. One actually hears the voice; one sees the face, body, and manner of the person who speaks. This individual is constantly on view, intruding his person and personality almost continuously into the narrative. If there is an interview with an important newsmaker, the story will depict the reporter, asking questions or listening and responding to answers, as well as the interviewee himself. Sometimes this personal narrator will make a passing reference to the process of covering the story. In fact, there is scarcely a moment in the television news story when the look, sound, manner, thought, and personality of the reporter-narrator is not visibly and audibly present. If the narrator of the newspaper story may be said to be a sort of disembodied zombie, then the narrator of television news is emphatically a real, flesh-and-blood person in all his uniqueness.

But not necessarily in all his fallible humanness. The television reporter, on camera, displays precious few weaknesses. His stance is easy and masterful, his voice commanding, his diction perfect; his lines are spoken flawlessly, his clothes wrinkle-free, custom-made, and color-coordinated, and his every hair is perfectly in (or out of, depending on the style) place. He may be a real person, but clearly he is playing a role, and in most cases (but not all: there is a measure of variety here) the posture he assumes is one of omniscience.

There is hardly an aspect of the scripting, casting, and staging of a television news program that is not designed to convey an impression of authority and omniscience. This can be seen most strikingly in the role of the anchorman—Walter Cronkite is the exemplar—who is positively god-like: he summons forth men, events, and images at will; he speaks in tones of utter certainty; he is the person with whom all things begin and end. But the omniscient pose is also adopted by reporters in the field. The "eyewitness" story format offers a particularly useful illustration: the reporter usually stands in front of the building or scene in question, his head and torso many times larger on the screen than the physical objects and persons involved in the actual events being reported. Throughout the report the actual occurrences are like putty in his masterful hands. He cuts from one shot to another; he stops the President in mid-sentence; he "voices over" images of kings, Congresses, wars, and citizens. At every point he conveys the subterranean but nonetheless powerful suggestion that the reporter is larger than life, that he literally as well as figuratively towers over the mere mortals whose doings and undoings he so easily and unerringly grasps and whose pretenses he sees through in an instant. Newsmen protest that this isn't at all what they have in mind; their concern is just to make the news visually interesting and intellectually coherent. Maybe so. But it doesn't really matter why they do it; the important thing is that they do it—and that, intentionally or not, they convey these suggestions of the TV newsman's omniscience to the viewer.

But most of all the television newsman's omniscience is apparent in what he says and how he says it. He is hardly one to limit and discipline himself in the manner of the newspaper narrator; he does not say less than he knows, nor is he willing to suggest by his silences, omissions, or ambiguities that there are things he does not know or cannot say for certain. To the contrary, he speaks authoritatively and self-confidently about everything that comes into his field of vision: men, events, motives, intentions, meanings, significances, trends, threats, problems, solutions—all are evidently within his perfect understanding, and he pronounces on them without any ifs, ands, or buts. To be sure, there are exceptions to this pose—TV newsmen such as John Chancellor who have begun to assume a stance not of omniscience but of a kind of sober, honest, self-critical, *reflexive* authoritativeness, in which the newsman not only says what he does know, but also makes clear his doubts, uncertainties, and the like, as well. These exceptions are few, however; most newsmen still pattern themselves after the example set by Walter Cronkite, who, despite the palpable absurdity of the notion that a definitive account of events is possible in principle, let alone in a 22-minute time-slot, continues to pronounce, God-like, the epitaph, "And that's the way it is . . ." at the end of each installment of *The CBS Evening News with Walter Cronkite.*

The personal and omniscient narrative of television journalism is noteworthy in a number of respects. It endows TV with an enormous added measure of moral, intellectual, and personal authority, as witness the fact that Walter Cronkite is among the nation's most admired and trusted men. It is hard to see how this narrative voice could be anything but a central cause of the enormous persuasive power of modern television. Yet it must also be said that the authoritativeness which TV newsmen pretend to is, in the end, a two-edged sword. For, omniscient or not, these newsmen are still identifiable on the screen as human beings, and it is therefore inevitable that, at some level, the audience is going to be aware that no one in real life ever knows so much or is so undoubting and intellectually self-assured, and that these television men are putting on a not entirely honest act. And when these men begin pronouncing *ex cathedra* on subjects about which the audience has strong feelings or substantial knowledge, the viewer is likely to be doubly irritated—first at the objectionable depiction of events, and second at the fraudulence and arrogance of the omniscient posture assumed by the man who conveys the objectionable depictions. Thus, ironically, each added increment of credibility which the omniscient narrator garners for television journalism automatically creates an equal increment of potential for "credibility gap" and public hostility toward television.

A second consequence arises out of this pose of omniscience as well: intellectual and political hubris. By the example its narrators set, by the "truths" they so confidently proclaim, and by the extraordinary power of the medium itself, television journalism encourages its viewers to entertain a badly inflated notion of how much it is possible to know and to do in the real world. By encouraging the sin of hubris, television journalism shows itself to be as unreliable, in the end, as the narrator of the newspaper news story, but for the opposite reason: not because it says less than it knows but because it says more.

IV.

Finally, television news differs from newspaper news in the vastly greater importance that TV attaches to spectacle. This is not so simply because television has such a large and sophisticated capacity for depicting the sights and sounds of events. At least as important is the fact that American television journalists have long since become institutionally committed to exploiting and emphasizing this special capability. They could—and in the early years of American television they did—follow, if only in a vague sort of way, the admirable model of the BBC and pay no more attention to the spectacular aspects of events than good newspapers do. But in American TV journalism today it is otherwise, to put it mildly. In almost any aspect of TV news that one might care to explore, one will find that considerations of pure spectacle count for much more than they do in newspaper journalism: in the choice of events to cover, in the allocation of resources among events, in the construction of events, in the choice of materials to illustrate stories, and perhaps above all in the selection of themes around which to build news stories.

In practical terms, this emphasis on spectacle is revealed in the television news organization's preoccupation with film, and especially with "good" film—i.e., film that clearly and dramatically depicts action, conflict, ritual, or color. Faced with a choice between two potentially newsworthy events, the American TV news organization will prefer, other things being equal, the one for which there is better film. What film they have for an event tentatively identified as newsworthy ordinarily guides, and in some instances may completely determine, the way the event is defined and the theme chosen for the story—a practice which can easily cause the story to misrepresent the situation as it really was. And in rare instances television news organizations have been known to "create" film, to stage spectacles for purposes of being filmed, in order to have something newsworthy to report. In newspapers, spectacle is but one of many competing and more completely coequal considerations, but in television it is a preoccupation. This preoccupation leads television journalism to give disproportionate coverage to events, or aspects of events, which are spectacular and spectacularly filmed.

This emphasis is noteworthy for a number of reasons. For one, it largely vitiates the unique flexibility and interpretive capabilities of the television news story, or rather it prevents their value from being fully realized. For under the influence of TV's passion for spectacle, the possibilities of the news story that could be used to counteract the inherent journalistic tendencies toward narrowness, literalness, short-sightedness, and the like, are instead exploited principally as a means of making news and events more visually interesting and emotionally stimulating than they are in real life. Second, the emphasis on spectacle tends to make TV journalism superficial in the literal sense of being fixated on the surface sights and sounds of events. Third, it powerfully reinforces the melodramatism inherent in American journalism, rendering television preeminently an instrument of symbolic politics. Fourth, the emphasis on spectacle lends additional forms of authority and interest to TV news: the interest and excitement which are characteristic of spectacle, and the largely specious but still quite real authority, or "credibility," of film as a mode of eyewitness observation. And finally the television emphasis on spectacle fixes the focus of TV journalism uniquely upon the ongoing drama of nationhood itself. Whereas newspapers focus on a diverse mass of specific events, television depicts something more directly thematic and melodramatic—the spectacle adorning the national dramas of the whole and the parts, of conflict and consensus, war and peace, danger and mastery, triumph and defeat, and so on.

V.

Though I don't pretend to know what all of them are, I am certain that there are many other differences between newspaper news and television news; the three discussed here illuminate only a small part of what is obviously a large and complex relationship. Yet even these elementary distinctions of structure, voice, and content do seem to establish the importance of looking into the relationship more deeply. For if what I have said thus far is true, then clearly the introduction of television journalism deserves to be considered an event of major consequence for all aspects of American life, and perhaps especially for American politics. Toqueville showed how the American political system rests on an uneasy balance between equality and liberty—or, as I would put it, between democracy and liberalism. On the analysis in these pages, the conclusion seems inescapable that whereas the effect of newspaper news is to sustain that balance, television news tends to upset it by reinforcing the egalitarian idea and by weakening liberalism.

Newspaper news tends to sustain the Tocquevillian balance by providing a great deal of precise information within a cognitive framework that is crude and nearly chaotic. It thus mobilizes public attention to public affairs (thereby performing an egalitarian-democratic function), while preserving to a significant extent the ability of each reader to choose for himself what to read and what to make of the data he encounters (the liberal idea). Thus there is an activation of public opinion as a whole (the democratic idea), but in behalf of no particular vision or objective save perhaps the ideal of individualism itself (the liberal idea). Through the newspaper, a single organization communicates directly with the electorate (the democratic impulse), but in a manner which suggests that no single coherent vision of public affairs is legitimate or even possible (the liberal idea). The newspaper sustains the Tocquevillian balance between democracy and liberalism, then, by incorporating both of these antagonistic ideas into its very conception of news. This practice is not without its disadvantages, to be sure. The liberal idea in particular, associated as it is with impersonal narrative and chaotic cognitive structure, creates more than its share of confusion. Yet as Tocqueville showed, the institutionalization of both ideas is necessary to the stability and legitimacy of the American regime—and if a bit of confusion or inelegance is the price we must pay for having them institutionalized in our media of public information, it seems a worthwhile bargain.

Television news, by contrast, incorporates no such admirable ambivalence. It is almost uniquely an expression of the democratic-egalitarian impulse. Television news is like newspaper news in that both mobilize public attention to public affairs and disseminate information—but there the similarities end. For television news is all mobilization; it seems utterly to lack the liberal, privatizing characteristics of print journalism—the discontinuities, the randomness, the ambiguities, and the diversity which give the ideal of individualism real substance. The television news emphasis on spectacle, its reliance on the single omniscient observer, and its commitment to the notion of a unified, thematic depiction of events, all make TV an extraordinarily powerful mobilizer of public attention and public opinion. The mobilization is organized around a single vision of public affairs promulgated by a single journalistic organization. Thus television news gives credence to the idea that there exists in America a single, coherent national agenda which can be perceived as such by any reasonable and well-intentioned person. Television news consequently lends a distinctive power and authority to the denigration of differences among us; it asserts that on the most fundamental level—that of deciding what is important enough to merit public attention—all Americans are essentially agreed and that wise public decisions can be reached through plebiscitarian consensus rather than through a system of institutions designed to represent and mediate differences among Americans.

Television news, in other words, is perhaps the most powerful centralizing-democratizing machine ever let loose in American society, a machine which, in its commitment to social unity and intellectual coherence, can scarcely avoid riding roughshod over the historic aspirations of liberalism—pluralism, diversity, localism, privacy, individualism, and untrammeled freedom for what is personal and idiosyncratic. So it is hard to imagine that the advent of television journalism is without significance for American politics and it is equally hard to believe that, in its current form, it is something that Americans should welcome with untroubled hearts.

Footnotes

1.   *There are other modes of newspaper writing, of course: the column, the editorial, the feature story, the news analysis. Each of these has its own characteristics. Here I am analyzing only the standard news story.*

2.   *I should emphasize that I am dealing here only with the filmed news story from a remote location. TV news programs also present "items" and "commentaries"—not many, usually, but some. These have their own characteristics and are not discussed in this paper.*

I don't see that, so far, anything terribly magic or terribly worrying has happened in relationship to television in the societies in which we live. One should remember that one of the most legitimate traditions of this country is skepticism of authority, with all that disquiet that skepticism can bring. We are now telling people more, and allowing them to know more about the situation. We may be telling them inadequately and badly and not telling them all about it. But we are, I think, telling more, and they are quite naturally becoming skeptical and coming to have a bad temper. I don't think that this is necessarily altogether a bad thing.

David Webster

American Political Legitimacy in an Era of Electronic Journalism: Reflections on the Evening News

Michael J. Robinson

As long as the economy holds out, liberal democracies get by—with or without political legitimacy.[1] But legitimacy is always an essential reserve. In the long run, democratic systems do not—cannot—survive monetary or social crises with institutions that lack the public's trust and respect. Thus in 1975 the instability of our economy, the inadequacy of our energy reserves and the incredulousness still surrounding our near impeachment, together, have forced many of us to doubt our capacity to preserve the Social Order—strange as this thought may be for those who have never once considered ourselves members of the American Ruling Class.

But these nightmares about Watergate, inflation, and gas lines are in some respects at least ten years too late. In terms of our legitimacy, Watergate admittedly did us no favors. According to the Harris poll, the percentage of our adult population expressing confidence in the executive branch (not the President)—once our most legitimate branch—hit a new low of 19 percent in November, 1973.[2] Following the "Saturday Night Massacre," a full 66 percent of the nation felt that they could, at best, trust the government "only some of the time" to do what is right.[3] But despite the very recent and precipitous decline in public confidence in the executive, his office and his government, the fact is that our inflation, our shortages, even our Watergate, all represent a wave, not the tide, in American politics. In truth, the tide has been moving inexorably since the late fifties—always on the ebb.

Until the sixties, the legitimacy of the American system had been forever growing—at least since the Depression. As late as 1958, whites and blacks—even in the year of Little Rock—showed identical and overwhelming

---

Michael Robinson is Assistant Professor of Politics at the Catholic University of America, Washington, D.C.

levels of commitment to and belief in our national political institutions.[4] But somewhere along the way, somewhere perhaps between the Kennedy and Johnson years, our political malaise began to emerge; it has abated only once since that time—during the first two "happy" years of the Nixon administration.[5]

Congress, the President and the Supreme Court have not been the only casualties of the sixties. As a nation we have also lost faith in ourselves as political entities. In fact, there is evidence to indicate that we came to doubt ourselves before coming to doubt our institutions; such was the depth of our loyalty. Since 1958 the proportion of Americans believing that they cannot even understand politics has virtually doubled.[6]

We have, in short, witnessed the slow and steady decline of two basic political commodities—belief in the worth and appropriateness of our governmental structures and belief in our own capacity to know and understand politics.

Not surprisingly, there are almost as many theories to explain this corrosion of spirit as there are theorists. There are theories of cyclical history—the Toynbee theme. There are theories based in Maslovian psychology. There are other, more straightforward theories too—theories which attribute our malaise to disconnected but dramatic events. But I suggest that there are now both data and logic which support a McLuhanist interpretation—that we are suffering from Videomalaise, that our doubts about ourselves and hostility toward our institutions would be far less severe were it not for the images we receive from the electronic media, more specifically, from network journalism.

In one respect this is an academic question. Our growing illegitimacy would not end tomorrow were we to shut down the networks in a fit of authoritarian pique. The effects may be so deeply embedded within the national psyche that daily choruses of the *Star-Spangled Banner* and *My Country 'Tis of Thee* sung by David Brinkley and Dan Rather would produce no remission whatever in our symptoms. I don't believe, however, that our case is inevitably a terminal one. Our condition is chronic, not critical. And I believe that we can find the roots of our condition first in 1956, the year in which the Huntley-Brinkley *Report* began, and especially in 1963, the year in which the two major networks, in pursuit of the public interest, developed the thirty-minute news program and began a new era of electronic journalism.

In the first section of this essay I will look at this supposition—that our current political pathology is a function of our television news system. And, having worked to establish a meaningful connection, I will try in the sections that follow to explain it, evaluate it from a moral and political perspective and suggest methods for coping with it.

Theories and Findings

My beliefs about television and its impact on legitimacy came to me only recently. Years ago, my own library research and my personal intuitions had led me to believe that television news, with its "liberal" bias, simply and mechanistically moved the society toward the left. But during the last three years I have found in several independent bits of research that the principal effect is not political liberalization; it is, instead, political frustration—political malaise. Having conducted a series of social experiments in the early seventies using *The Selling of the Pentagon,* I discovered that the general response to so controversial a program was neither a markedly increasing disdain for the military nor a markedly decreasing credibility for CBS, the parent of the program. The general response was an increasing belief that the viewer himself couldn't come to grips with the political issues involved.[7] After seeing *The Selling* my white, Christian, midwestern subjects left the viewing studio feeling frustrated and politically emasculated—politically impotent, so to speak. I found a similar reaction—a reaction based in frustration—among two groups of randomly-selected Oregonians, following their own voluntary exposure to the televised Watergate hearings.[8] Respondents came away from that experience with an increasing hostility towards government and an increasing sense of personal perplexity.[9] But I use these studies only as a backdrop. In this essay I prefer to focus upon other work with which I have been most recently involved. These findings are, I confess, only partly mine; the data belong to the Survey Research Center at the University of Michigan. Therefore, although the calculations are all mine, the respondents are eternally theirs and I thank them for the loan. *178081*

My recent work with television has forced me to build a yet untested, theory concerning the growth of political illegitimacy. I have begun to envision a two-stage process in which television journalism, with its constant emphasis on social and political conflict, its high credibility, its powerful audio-visual capabilities and its epidemicity, has caused the more vulnerable viewers first to doubt their own understanding of their political system. (The major institutions are, after all, too preciously regarded to disdain at first.) But once these individuals have passed this initial stage they enter a second phase in which personal denigration continues and in which a new hostility toward politics and government also emerges. Having passed through both stages of political cynicism, these uniquely susceptible individuals pass their cynicism along to those who were, at the start, less attuned to television messages and consequently less directly vulnerable to televisual malaise. (Public opinion polls may prove to be the most effective carrier for those who are not directly connected to or dependent upon TV news.)

All this is theory, of course. But the theory fits nicely with the findings from the experimental work I have done in the past.[10] To demonstrate that the theory fits with national survey data as well, I offer the following set of findings from the 1968 election study, a national survey conducted by the Michigan Survey Research Center, in Ann Arbor.[11]

I divided all the respondents in this survey into three distinct groups. Those individuals who relied upon something other than television for their political information in 1968 were placed in Group A; those who relied principally upon television were placed in Group B; and those who followed politics *only* through television were placed in Group C. Having constructed such a "variable"—a variable with three distinct levels of television dependency—I checked to see if those who were dependent upon television were different, politically speaking, from those who were not.

If the theory of televisual malaise were to have any validity, one should have expected from all these operations to find, at a minimum, two things: (1) some correlation, however modest, between the level of television dependency and attitudes towards one's own political self-esteem, and (2) some correlation, presumably smaller than that above, between the level of dependency and attitudes toward political institutions. (One might also expect to find, were there data from earlier elections, that the first set of correlations—correlations between the level of dependency and political self-esteem—would appear at an earlier point in time than would the others.)

Although the findings do not match perfectly with the theory, there is enough correspondence to merit further investigation, as well as an explanation. A more stringent test of the theory is in progress, and the explanation of the theory begins on page 105.

I have selected three items which in some ways tap some of the dimensions of public opinion which are relevant to any discussion of legitimacy. I have selected these three because they deal with the two stages on the road to illegitimacy—political self-doubt and political cynicism directed against our institutions. I have also chosen them because they tend to fit the theory rather well. But many of the items I checked which are not reported here fit the theory almost as well.

Two of the three items are of one type: Respondents were asked whether or not they agreed with a series of political statements. The statements were:

1. Sometimes politics and government seem so complicated that a person like me can't really understand what's going on.

2. Generally speaking, those we elect to Congress in Washington lose touch with the people pretty quickly.

The third statement was different in that it provided three possible choices:

3. Do you think that quite a few people running the government are a little crooked, not very many are, or do you think hardly any of them are at all?

The first item was specifically used to assess the individual's attitude toward himself as a political entity. The second item—about Congress—was the one direct test of institutional responsiveness. The third item was a bridge, asking not about a specific institution but all the individuals involved, collectively, in the government.

The findings are presented in toto in tables 1, 2 and 3. In general, the pattern I had anticipated emerged. Even when examining respondents with similar levels of education, the greater the dependency upon television, the greater the personal confusion and estrangement from government. Those who rely upon television in following politics are more confused and more cynical than those who do not. And those who rely totally upon television are the most confused and cynical of all. The differences among the groups run generally between 10 percent and 15 percent. When looking at respondents with a similar level of education the differences diminish, but they do not disappear. Interestingly enough, the differences are greatest among those with a high school education—the middle-status Americans—a finding which fits well with the conventional wisdom concerning "the real America" during the last ten years.

There is one other bit of evidence which fits the theory. In general, there are greater differences between the groups on the items concerning personal political capacity than on items dealing with governmental institutions. Obviously, this does not prove that the process is, in fact, two-staged. But this finding is consistent with that interpretation.

In general, these findings do not "prove" anything. When two variables correlate, one cannot infer that one causes the other. In fact, some will undoubtedly argue that my findings show precisely the reverse of what I suggest—that those who are already frustrated are merely moved to watch television, instead of the other way around. (More on that later.) For now we should remember that these variables cannot tell us much about the sequence of events. Did personal frustration really precede frustration with the institutions? These data cannot give a definitive answer. Nor do these data speak unequivocally to the basic theory—that television produces political malaise. There are holes here. But we should remember too that the findings run in the right direction. The relationships, if weak, are as predicted in most cases, even with controls for other variables. And we should also remember that the TV variable we use is a very poor one—one which does not really convey the amount of exposure, only the comparative amount. Furthermore, there is no specific item about "network" television. But one has to use the data available to him or to her. As it stands now, I am planning my own research project to get at this question of television malaise more directly. But for the moment I hope that these findings will at least set the stage for the essay which follows.

There are, however, two last points to be made in defense of this assumed tie between television exposure and prevailing political ethos. First, all

TABLE 1

Respondent's opinion as to
whether or not he can understand politics

	GROUP A Those not relying on television	GROUP B Those relying on television	GROUP C Those relying *only* on television
Percentage who cannot *understand*	63% (417)	71% (693)	91% (130)

Controlling for education level of respondent

	Those not relying on television	Those relying on television	Those relying *only* on television
Percentage who cannot *understand*			
Less than 8 grades	83% (23)	87% (67)	97% (30)
Grades 8 thru 11	82% (102)	84% (223)	96% (51)
Grade 12	62% (129)	70% (211)	82% (39)
Some college	51% (77)	60% (110)	71% (7)
College	54% (60)	38% (59)	100% (1)
College +	33% (27)	58% (24)	100% (2)

these relationships exist not only in the 1968 data but in the 1964 data and the 1960 data as well. Before that time there was no relationship between television dependency and one's opinions about his or her political worth or the worth of our political institutions.[12] This dividing line between 1956 and 1960 is a fascinating one, one which suggests that the coming of the Huntley-Brinkley *Report* may have initiated the coming of a new era of political estrangement. It is at least an interesting point to consider.

   The other point is more procedural than substantive. Agreed that the findings I offer here do not set the world on fire. When combined with findings from my other research they become a little more convincing. Even when these

TABLE 2

Respondent's opinion as to
whether or not government leaders are crooked

	GROUP A	GROUP B	GROUP C
	Those not relying on television	Those relying on television	Those relying *only* on television
Percent believing "quite a few" are crooked	21% (401)	27% (676)	34% (115)

Controlling for educational level of respondent

	Those not relying on television	Those relying on television	Those relying *only* on television
Percent believing "quite a few" are crooked			
Less than 8 grades	24% (21)	26% (65)	43% (21)
Grades 8 thru 11	26% (97)	29% (214)	35% (46)
Grade 12	22% (126)	29% (207)	32% (38)
Some college	20% (74)	29% (108)	14% (7)
College	17% (58)	19% (59)	*
College +	8% (25)	17% (23)	50% (2)

*No valid codes.

findings are taken alone, it is amazing that any of the differences between the three groups occur, given the inherent weakness of the procedures used to uncover them.

But, despite all the weaknesses and all the caveats, I hope that these findings will not be dismissed too facilely. Social scientists and journalists

TABLE 3

Respondent's view as to
whether or not Congressmen lose touch
with constituents after election

	GROUP A Those not relying on television	GROUP B Those relying on television	GROUP C Those relying *only* on television
Percent believing Congressman does lose touch with constituents	47% (402)	57% (675)	68% (122)

Controlling for educational level of respondent

	Those not relying on television	Those relying on television	Those relying *only* on television
Percent believing Congressman does lose touch with constituents			
Less than 8 grades	71% (21)	75% (65)	76% (25)
Grades 8 thru 11	58% (97)	66% (216)	69% (48)
Grade 12	46% (127)	54% (217)	62% (39)
Some college	51% (76)	44% (108)	71% (7)
College	29% (56)	46% (56)	100% (1)
College +	32% (25)	30% (23)	50% (2)

frequently discount theories such as mine—theories that even hint of a McLuhanist persuasion. Much of their skepticism is warranted, but at least some grows in the soil of an intellectual ethnocentrism. Social scientists may not see or admit the impact of television because they themselves are in its midst. Social scientists are especially vulnerable to this weakness—to deny an effect which may exist in them as well as in their subjects and respondents. But those who deny the possibility of any effects and plead their own sophistication as defense may in themselves prove to be the last to know what is happening around them. We have all had our perceptions of the world molded by television news, no matter how tightly we hold our copies of the *Times* or the *Post* to our breasts or our minds. I might even go so far as to suggest that the individuals who create the *Times* and the *Post* have even been affected by the images the networks provide.

So for the remainder of this piece I prefer to assume that the coincidence between the growth of television journalism and the growth in political illegitimacy is not coincidental. Nothing in these data, or in any data I have collected during the last four years, moves me very far from my convictions about television news and the state of our world. Therefore, I will suppose this hypothetical relationship between television and our political ethos to be real from this point on. And in the next three sections I will attempt to explain that relationship by analyzing (a) the audience for, (b) the content within, and (c) the personnel of the network news system.

The Inadvertent Television News Audience

The enormity of the network news audience is undeniable. With virtually each passing year the audience for television journalism becomes larger and more television-dependent.

In 1973 ABC commissioned a Nielsen Survey and discovered that the three nightly news programs reached 50 million homes in the average month and 46 million homes in the average week—71 percent of all homes.[13] And these figures, although probably somewhat inflated, represented, respectively, a 7 percent and 9 percent increase from 1972, suggesting the imperiousness of television journalism.

Along with the absolute size of the news audience, dependency on TV news has also increased. The Roper poll has, with tedious regularity, demonstrated that television, year by year, strengthens its position as the most-preferred medium.[14] In my own research I find a clear majority (56 percent) following national politics principally through television and another 10 percent following only through television.[15]

However, the absolute size of the audience, in and of itself, is not the most important factor. The first crucial factor in understanding television's impact upon legitimacy is the abnormality of shape and composition of the television audience.

I begin with an assumption—that any increase in available political information within a society, especially a libertarian society, will probably increase, to some degree, the level of political frustration or disaffection. If this were not a high probability, one would expect much less concern with the once radical notion that the press should be essentially free—an idea that is, after all, rejected by the vast majority of the governments and, I dare say, people of our world. (CBS News itself discovered that as late as March, 1970, 55 percent of the American public felt that when our government believes national interest is involved it should be able to stop any and all news reports.[16])

Clearly, the potential effect of increasing information does not always materialize. During World War II, one guesses, our media expanded and presumably so did the availability of information. But under those extraordinary circumstances the increase in absolute level of information probably *decreased* the level of political disquiet. Information in a democracy need not always produce disaffection. Nonetheless, the increase of information in an open system of media carries with it a marked potential for creating political anxiety. And it appears as if the television news "system," which began in the mid-fifties, has helped to realize the potential anxiety. In fact, one might argue that public affairs television has so profoundly distorted the general historical pattern of informational expansion that the realization of that potential has become and is a certainty.

When Latin was translated into common tongues during the Renaissance, when print was invented, when the penny press emerged, there was an obvious expansion in the availability of information—political and otherwise. Generally, the expansion was downward through the social strata. But the increase in audience was biased in favor of the upper classes. Changing from Latin to English increased media exposure, but more for the nobles than the serfs. The adoption of print also increased the level of exposure for all groups, but the increase was greater among the social, economic and political elites. So it was always—at least until radio and television. But the electronic media have made the process of communication almost effortless. After all, it is easier to hear than to read, and easier to see than to hear. As a consequence, the electronic media—especially television—have produced an audience different from the Mass Audience of the eighteenth, nineteenth, or even early twentieth centuries; they have produced, instead, the Inadvertent Audience as well. The Inadvertent Audience is that large, amorphous portion within the Mass Audience, that portion which will *not read* the news of the day but which is willing *to listen to* or *watch* the news if the listening or watching is entertaining. Obviously, the Inadvertent Audience has transformed the old Mass Audience, making it larger than before. But the Inadvertent Audience has done more than merely increase the size of the Mass Audience. The Inadvertent Audience differs from the Mass Audience qualitatively as well. The new audience, unlike the old, receives its politically relevant information through a wholly passive process—one in which the viewer literally falls into the audience. Similar notions about accidental audiences must have tormented the German aristocrats when Gutenberg made possible not only the penny press but the pandering entrepreneur and yellow journalism as well. Every new medium is, after all, said to be the end—the ultimate disequilibrating social force; and I confess to my own temporocentric bias. But in some respects the audience for the pamphlets of Paine and the Manifesto by Marx were of a different—and far less inadvertent—character. All other things being equal, their audiences were even *less* volatile than those which television provides. Television, in essence, provides an audience which is the most likely of all to realize the potential political discord which accompanies an informational expansion.

Why should all this be true? Why is the Inadvertent Audience so vulnerable to the effects we have already documented? Why? Because television builds an audience with few of the self-regulating processes which the print media have always provided—self-regulating processes which have, until now, permitted government and free press to live together, even if the relationship were strained.

An early disciple of James Madison, writing in defense of a free press, would, no doubt, have looked beyond the inherent dangers of tabloidism by pointing to the most important, internal check on the power of print—the direct relationship between class and propensity to read. At every other time, with every other medium, this relationship has served as a political filter. The aristocrat paid more attention to the written event than the farmer, the capitalist more than the worker. Information was obtained more frequently by those who could and would pay the price—in time, as well as in coin. John Robinson has shown how vibrant and how ironic the relationship between social status and exposure to the print media can be, even in the United States.

> *People with a college education, when compared to their country-men with less than a high school education, are not only twenty times as likely to regularly read sophisticated commentary magazines and fifteen times as likely to read a general news magazine, they are also three times as likely to read a pictorial and general interest magazine . . . the best known of these magazines is often referred to as 'the magazine for those who can't think. . .'*[17]

But today the once immutable and universal law of exposure has been overturned. Not only are the less-educated no less likely to watch television journalism, they are more likely to do so! The data in Table 4, taken from a very recent study completed in Minneapolis and based upon diaries kept by viewers, show that the lowest educational stratum watches more television news than the highest—not only in terms of absolute minutes, but also in percent of total viewing time.[18] Neither William Randolph Hearst nor Henry Luce, at their best or at their worst, could achieve anything like this. Such is the nature of television's Inadvertent Audience.

An 18th century liberal would, one presumes, have based his case for maintaining both a free press and the social order upon the anticipated intellectual indolence of the rabble; the words to ignite the passions of the nonaristocratic population would never be read. This being a principal defense for freeing the press, the Inadvertent Audience must produce some serious anxieties for the Madisonian-based proponents of the First Amendment. Even for those who are more contemporary in their thinking, the Inadvertent Audience is still an unsettling reality.

Until the coming of the television news system, there was a second internal mechanism that could help reconcile press freedom with a commitment to preserve the social order. Had Madison had the chance to read Katz and Lazarsfeld he would have discovered that these two patently nonaristocratic sociologists had found another argument for allowing an independent media within a free society. Katz and Lazarsfeld realized that the mass audience was really two audiences in one, that political information did not pass from source to mass directly.[19] A wall of Opinion Leaders stood between them, Opinion Leaders who would invariably interpret the original message.

While nobody could guarantee that the opinion leaders would be more sympathetic to and supportive of the prevailing institutions of the period, there was some evidence and some speculation to suggest that they were.[20] At the very least, the Opinion Leaders were a buffer between any disconcerting information and the potentially disconcerted reader or listener. Consequently, in most cases this two-step flow of communication between the media and the public could serve to militate against the types of effects that a free press might be expected to engender.

But in this instance as well, television journalism has reversed the traditional process of communication. The two-step flow has dried to a trickle.[21] Since the mid-fifties the networks have apparently managed to bypass the Opinion Leaders and deal directly with the Mass Audience and the Inadvertent Audience. By circumventing the Opinion Leaders, television has "subverted" another source of mediation between the source and the target, another self-regulating mechanism.

Both the obsolescence of the two-step model and the unique composition of the television Inadvertent Audience are, of course, the consequence of the tremendous pulling power of commercial television, a medium which manages to consume more than 30 percent of all our free time in America.[22] But there is still one more consequence of the magnetism of commercial television which is relevant to us in explaining the vulnerability of the network news audience.

Commercial television news has actually reduced the amount of contact with the other informational media (i.e., the competing news media). Having established itself as a serious journalistic enterprise, television journalism has managed to supplant other news media in popularity. Those who once read the news with less than complete dedication have begun to accept network journalism as an ample dosage of political information. The networks have become the only, as well as the first, source of information for millions of Americans. This is not a case for snobbishness; I have never believed that reading is, per se, the greater, purer good. But by unintentionally persuading viewers that they are informed by following television news—by narcoticizing viewers and

TABLE 4

Actual TV viewing habits by level of education in Minneapolis in 1970 (expressed in percentages of total minutes of TV watched)*

	EDUCATION			
PROGRAM TYPE	0-8 yrs.	9-11 yrs.	12 yrs.	1-4 yrs. College
Comedy-variety	27	25	27	23
Movies	16	19	21	20
Action	17	17	16	15
Sports	6	9	8	13
Light music	11	11	10	8
Light drama	1	2	3	2
News	20	15	14	17
Information and public affairs	2	2	2	2
Heavy drama	–	–	–	1
Religion	1	1	–	–
Heavy music	–	–	–	–
Base (Minutes): 100 percent =	41,535	39,540	163,150	73,740
N (number of viewers) =	(38)	(38)	(176)	(76)

*Taken from Bower's Television and the Public, *(1973), p. 132.*

unwittingly justifying their reliance upon one medium—the networks have undermined, to some degree, a third mediating factor in the communications process. The networks have, in the last ten years, undermined the tendency to supplement one medium with another. For much of the population—a growing percentage—the only supplementation of information is *among networks,* not between media. Given the subtle types of nonpolitical bias which exist at the networks (see the following section), this is a significant development in the process of political communication.

On the other hand, to some people in my audience—all those who have chosen to read this essay—these notions about the size, shape and composition of the Inadvertent Audience may seem a little boring, if not a little contrived. Despite the appearance of banality, however, these notions are fundamental. To understand the broad-based, denigrating effects of television news, one must remember that commercial television has produced a new system of political communication, a system in which some of the most important and self-contained mechanisms through which free media and political authority are reconciled have been jeopardized. Commercial television has not only produced an audience for television journalism which is unique in history; it has also produced an audience which is basic to all of us in trying to understand the flow of political information in the United States.

American television has, in short, assembled a national news audience that is at one and the same time disproportionately drawn from the lower end of the sociological spectrum, more likely to obtain its information directly from the source, and increasingly more willing to satisfy its total desire for information through only one medium. In fact, no one single factor helps explain television malaise more fundamentally than these unique, if relatively obvious, characteristics of the Inadvertent Audience. The Inadvertent Audience is a necessary condition for my theory.

But the uniqueness of the audience is just that—a necessary, not a sufficient condition for explaining the effects of network television upon our political institutions and our political ethos. If there were strict, authoritarian controls imposed upon news content, there would be no such effects. But given the content provided by the network news organizations, the effects are more readily understood.

The Nonpartisan Biases of Television News

Given the general tenor of American journalism, if the actual content of television journalism were identical to that of the print media (i.e., if both used identical copy) we might expect television journalism to produce more political cynicism and estrangement than print—simply because television reaches more people. But the major media do not present the same copy. They each provide different emphases, different directions; each medium has its own inherent set of biases. Television journalism, in short, presents images of our society and our politics that are different from those of the print media or even radio, and these differences represent a type of bias.

Despite the conventional wisdom, the biases inherent in television news are not overwhelmingly, or even substantially, politically partisan. Edith Efron's assertions that the networks produce news that invariably supports the "Liberal-left-Democratic Axis of opinion" is not so much wrong as ill-conceived and misinterpreted.

Political imbalance does exist within the press corps, both electronic and print. During my own limited experience with the press coverage of the impeachment process, for example, I witnessed an almost consensual expression of opinion favoring Nixon's impeachment among members of the corps. (Incidentally, that consensus preceded the Saturday Night Massacre.) One of the principal network correspondents assigned directly to the impeachment inquiry demonstrated, in private but audibly, a serious hostility to and a partisan contempt for then-President Nixon and his administration. However, very little of that political bias came through during this correspondent's nightly telecasts. (Indeed, in the one incident in which this particular correspondent was forced to choose between his own feelings about a successful impeachment and his personal commitment to report news as he had heard it, despite its implications for impeachment—the incident involved Peter Rodino's alleged prediction on the vote for impeachment within the Judiciary Committee—he chose the latter course, the professional course, albeit reluctantly.)

But, despite a relatively objective public performance on impeachment, the networks would be hard-pressed to make a case that there is no partisan imbalance within the minds and hearts of the press corps, even if the networks swear that the biases remain confined to the minds and hearts of their correspondents when the news is reported. In 1968, after interviewing the technical staff, executives and correspondents at NBC News, Edward Epstein concluded that the overwhelming majority of the correspondents at NBC thought of themselves as liberals or held positions on public issues which Epstein regarded as liberal.[23] Evidence that is perhaps more poignant comes from a *Playboy* interview with Walter Cronkite which took place as late as 1973. Knowing that his remarks in *Playboy* could boomerang, Cronkite, when asked about the alleged left-of-center orientation of television newsmen, responded:

> . . *Well, certainly liberal, and possibly left of center as well. I would have to accept that. . . . I think that being a liberal, in the true sense, is being nondoctrinaire, nondogmatic, noncommitted to a cause—but examining each case on its merits. Being left of center is another thing; it's a political position. I think most newspapermen by definition have to be liberal; if they're not liberal, by my definition of it, then they can hardly be good newspapermen. If they're preordained dogmatists for a cause, then they can't be very good journalists; that is, if they carry it into their journalism.*[24]

Cronkite's remarks point up two truths—that the television newsperson tends to be a liberal but that biases in reporting are not partisan liberal, or as Cronkite calls them, left of center. In fact, despite the overwhelming Democratic, "liberal" orientation among members of the network news corps, according to one still-unpublished analysis of the 1972 election, all three networks—ABC, CBS, NBC—reported the Nixon-Agnew candidacies more favorably (actually, less unfavorably) than the McGovern-Eagleton-Shriver candidacies.[25] This finding alone requires that we posit a more sophisticated interpretation of the type of content which network news organizations provide, an interpretation which transcends the relatively superficial conspiracy theories popularized by former Vice-President Agnew.

Basically, the images of television journalism are determined far more by the organizational needs of the networks and the organizational perceptions of the national audience than by the generally nonideological political opinions of the network journalists themselves. (Epstein says the correspondents are fundamentally nonpolitical in their thinking.)

Beyond their own commitment to reporting news, according to Epstein, the news organizations must do four things in order to maintain themselves and expand their budgets: (1) satisfy the corporation by cutting unnecessary news costs (Jack Schneider used to complain that fixed costs for news were reasonable but "unscheduled" news was hurting the CBS rate of return); (2) satisfy the parent organization by maintaining an audience, inadvertent or otherwise; (3) satisfy the affiliates by holding the audience and avoiding controversy over fundamentals; (4) keep the FCC away from the affiliates by presenting "balanced" news items and items which are of national interest. It is out of this rather cynical collection of obligations—not the liberal predispositions of the news departments—that the TV images of our society come, and have come, since the mid-fifties. It is their organizational needs which produce a content at ABC, NBC and CBS that is essentially the same—despite the varying political opinions of the people who run those three greatly similar organizations.

The Thematic Bias: The first characteristic which flows from the obligations of the organization is the thematic news report. More than any other major news source—except local TV news, a world unto itself—the networks have come to appreciate the Short Story. If one looks closely at the last 15 minutes of the evening news, one finds a virtual compendium of politically relevant essays. The Short Story is invaluable to the network news organization. It tends to hold the audience, especially the Inadvertent Audience (given the criteria for a successful news show, members of the Inadvertent Audience are just as valuable to the networks as any other).

The thematic Short Story, has, however, become more than a simple pattern of evening news. The entire network news organization is geared to thematic presentation. In 1969 and 1973 I took the opportunity to quiz my undergraduate students about the then most-recent Democratic presidential primary in New Hampshire. The quiz was simple enough—who won? In both years the majority of the class was wrong, choosing McCarthy in 1968 and

McGovern in 1972. Inevitably it was the networks which were the source of the misinformation. This is not to say that the networks ever gave the wrong information. They merely gave the wrong impression—thematically. The misrepresentation was inherent in the TV image of the New Hampshire campaign, not the campaign itself. Perhaps more than any other medium, network television was forced, because of obligations one and two, in both elections, to build a horse race, complete with a phantom winner. As the undisputed major source of information about the primaries, television was probably the most effective among all the media in convincing viewers and Democrats that losers were winners in New Hampshire, as well as in several other states.

But the theme of the dark horse does not tie us directly to television malaise. At best, it ties us to the crucial role the networks have played in confusing Democratic rank-and-file during the last two campaigns—a confusion that was far more serious than that produced by Dwight Chapin or Donald Segretti. But the same straining for story line has come to be the *sine qua non* of the evening news. Given the network perceptions of the news audience, themes must be simple and interesting: venality, social discord, bureaucratic bungling, and, especially, the good old days. This is the repertoire from which so much of the soft news is chosen. The hard news is usually allowed to take care of itself.

In one respect the theme of social discord is extraordinarily well-suited to television. It is a hook from which one can hang a good deal of sensational film footage. But, contrary to conventional wisdom, the networks do not include more violent news than the print media,[26] the reason being that most violence is unplanned and cannot be readily filmed.

When there is planned violence, or violence that takes place through an extended period of time, the networks can be expected to move enormous amounts of equipment to the staging area. The coverage of the battle of Wounded Knee was a finest hour—in terms of television needs. But, if there is nothing of that nature transpiring, nothing to meet the theme of social discord, the networks can shift to closely-related themes. Intragovernmental conflict is another theme that the networks continue to utilize. Senators fighting with businessmen, bureaucrats, each other, is a popular theme; so are governmental unresponsiveness and governmental laxity. David Brinkley, Hughes Rudd and Charles Kuralt have virtually built their television careers on the theme that our government functions badly and that it used to work far better than it does now.

The themes which the networks offer are predominantly negative.[27] That alone would suggest that our opinions about our government, our society and ourselves would tend not to be positive. But the more important aspect of thematic reporting is inherent conflict, either personal or organizational. My own experiments with viewers suggest that this personal and institutional conflict, so appropriate and essential to thematic reporting, is profoundly disturbing to the audience, especially the Inadvertent Audience. The news organization and the journalist may believe that conflict between Senators or business leaders or bureaucrats is good copy; perhaps it is. But among the inadvertent viewers I suggest that this copy takes on a different and more profound meaning. The general effects are, I surmise, not only sustained viewing but growing political estrangement and a desire to return to a bygone era of political purity and decency, an era which is undoubtedly overly-romanticized by the networks and all the mass media.

The Nonquantitative Bias: In their eagerness to provide palatable news, the networks not only construct thematic reports, they construct stories which are essentially qualitative bits of information taken from more substantial stories or items. The brief items may contain hard evidence—stock quotations, inflation statistics, unemployment figures, etc., but the longer stories do not.[28] My own experience with local television underscores the problem. Having spent three months on a study of the impact of the Watergate hearings on local public opinion, I made my findings available to the local newspaper and a local television station. The newspaperwoman I dealt with demanded to see my figures, checked my calculations and even asked about my sampling procedures. In the newspaper article which subsequently appeared all the information was there—the tables, the procedures, the conclusions. In stark contrast, the TV journalist who was assigned to the story asked me not to discuss the procedures or the findings—just my interpretations and the implications. So when I appeared I discussed everything but the facts of the case.

Ironically, both "stories" contained approximately the same number of words, but the TV report was clearly a story with less information. It was qualitative assessment, from start to finish. Not surprisingly, the television story was more dramatic, more unqualified. (I confess that I found myself straining to make my study sound more significant than I otherwise believed it was. The medium carries such temptations.)

The nonquantitative bias apparently exists at the network level as well. Again personal experience suggests that this bias has two roots—the widely-held belief that the audience does not want quantitative evidence and the self-realization that the journalist himself can't cope with data. I had the opportunity to present those same findings about the effects of the Senate Watergate hearings to a network correspondent who had actually covered the hearings for one of the networks. The correspondent showed interest in my work and asked that I send along a copy of the study. However, the correspondent, who possessed impressive academic credentials, also asked that I carefully explain the findings, because survey data presented in tabularized form were too hard to comprehend.

Obviously, television news cannot become a series of lectures based on quantitative data. Even the *New York Times* is, at base, a collection of anecdotes. But the nonquantitative bias—the anti-quantitative bias—is more intense on the part of the networks than it is with the other prestigious news organizations. And, although we have come to take this particular form of bias for granted, almost as inevitable, this bias may have greater significance than many of the others in explaining the effects of television journalism.

As most radicals seem to recognize, qualitative stories characteristically paint the society more negatively than quantitative research does. Quantitative research generally offers a more optimistic picture—or, at the very least, a less vivid one. In the *Washington Post* in February, 1974, for example, we find a lengthy front-page summary of an OMB report on several social indicators in the United States.[29] The overwhelming majority of the indicators pointed upward during the last decade, indicating a continual improvement in the human condition. As well as can be ascertained, the report was not mentioned in any of the evening news programs at any time during the next week, despite its prominence in both the *Post* and its conspicuous inclusion in the *Times*.[30]

Edith Efron might argue that the report was not included in the network broadcast because it put the administration in a good light, at least indirectly. I suggest that this is not the reason at all. Neither the *Post* nor the *Times* has enthusiastically endorsed the Nixon or Ford administrations more frequently than the networks have. The report simply contained too much information, not too much positive information but too much tabularized —quantitative—information.

But looking beyond the motives which explain the cause for the omission, we need to face the more important question of the effects. Is it not possible that the networks, by developing a strong predilection for news which is nonquantitative, have produced a package of bizarre sensational anecdotes— anecdotes which themselves produce, as a by-product, a sense of political estrangement? George Gerbner and Larry Cross have already demonstrated that heavy reliance on all types of television programming is associated with distorted perceptions of social reality, in part because television provides such anecdotal and extraordinary images of society.[31] And it is hard to deny that the networks have a marked propensity for nonquantitative, anecdotal, image-based news. If one can suppose that the effect of this unwitting bias is a popular perception of society which is more imaginary than real, and more cynical than deserved, one can begin to comprehend at least one meaning to the McLuhanist dictum that the medium is the message.

The Bias of Artificial Balance: To insure a cooperative relationship between themselves and their local affiliates, the networks must present news stories that are "balanced"—in other words, stories that do not violate the Fairness Doctrine. The doctrine requires that local broadcasters (affiliates) provide an opportunity for alternate points of view. Because the networks operate their own affiliates and because they must answer to the affiliates which they do not own, the networks abide by the provisions of the doctrine as scrupulously as the local stations. Ironically, this adds one more unique and disquieting dimension to the television news program—the bias of artificial balance.

To meet their obligation the journalists and producers always include "both" points of view (in the eyes of the FCC the world is always a dichotomy). While this procedure ensures that news will not persuade viewers to accept a point of view—the balanced story is, in most circumstances, the less effective story[32] —it also ensures the inevitable depiction of disputation and conflict. Sometimes the journalist is obliged to invent the second point of view, the conflicting point of view. But in either case this obligation to develop two sides to every story places legitimate organs of government or respectable segments of society at odds. The networks strain to find a credible "other side" and generally they do.

Under some circumstances the networks may omit the "opposing viewpoint." By 1972, for example, there was little network journalism that could be regarded as supportive of our continued involvement in Vietnam. And if we can accept the findings of Ernest Lefever's newest book (and in part I accept them), by 1973 there was very little indeed on the evening news to dispute the alleged advantages in Soviet-American detente.[33] But these are exceptional cases. The Fairness Factor is a way of life in network news.

The result of all this "fairness" is a mixed blessing. All the balance implies disputation. Under these provisions of fairness, programming may be less likely to persuade, but it is also more likely to confuse or irritate. For this reason the bias of artificial balance may explain why the people who rely on television are totally convinced that politics is not only venal but also indecipherable. And again the networks have produced, wholly inadvertently in this case, another source for Videomalaise.

The Federal Bias: The American communications system has been and remains remarkably decentralized. The United States has no national daily. The closest we come, ironically, is the *Wall Street Journal.* Consequently, until the advent of radio and television, national news was a pastiche of wire service reports and bureau copy. But network television has changed both the tenor and pattern of news about national politics.

This predilection for monitoring life along the Potomac is easily explained. Central locating not only reduces the cost of news production, it also satisfies the local affiliates, who are themselves obliged to carry a proportion of national news. In early 1973, even before the impeachment process began, more than 40 percent of the network news items were out of Washington—four times the number out of New York.[34] This federal bias is, I suggest, much more significant than might first be apparent.

For one thing, the network national bias has totally re-routed the path toward the Presidency; what was once a regional or state process is now centered in D.C., thanks to the networks. Between 1900 and 1956 only 7% of those nominated to become President were Senators. But since 1956 only incumbent or former Senators have managed to run for President or Vice President, Agnew being the one exception.

More importantly, the federal bias has also contributed to our growing sense of political illegitimacy, again in an indirect and almost imperceptible way. I believe that there is an iron law of media exposure, a law no less deterministic—and no less dismal—in its implications than the iron laws of wages or population. The iron law of media requires that in nations where news is produced commercially and independently, the level (or branch) of government which receives the greatest emphasis will, in the long run, also experience the greatest public disdain. For several decades local government was the focal point for our localized, independent media, and it was local government which sustained the greatest public criticism. But network television has shifted the focus of daily news almost totally to national, to Washington, events. Again, given the types of messages provided by the networks, this focus has, in ten years, made national politics the most suspect. Stated as law, one ultimately finds that the locus of government which gains attention eventually gains opprobrium. This has been the case with our federal government since the late fifties. (See Table 5)

Interestingly enough, the new and intense focus on Washington has not caused a reduction in the absolute amount of local news coverage; television journalism has merely changed the proportions given to each type. One actually finds more coverage at all levels and, presumably, all branches of government than one found ten or even five years ago. And, as one would predict—were he or she to believe in the iron law of media exposure—public opinion concerning local government has, over the last few years, become more negative (Table 5). But, having received proportionally less attention, local governments have shown a slower rate of increase in public disdain.

It would not be difficult to demonstrate a final case for the iron law—to demonstrate that the coverage of state news has also increased with time, but at a rate slower than that of either local or national news, and to demonstrate that the increase in disapproval of state government has been, as expected, slower than that of the other two levels of government (again, Table 5). In short, television has increased its coverage of all three levels of government, and consequently all three levels of government have experienced an increase in public disapproval. The absolute increase in disapproval appears to be directly related to the absolute increase in the attention provided by the media.

All this implies that the federal bias, which is so severe and so intrinsic to network journalism, has, in one more paradoxical process, made the national government more visible, more salient, and, as a consequence, more disreputable in the public mind.

All told, the biases of television are subtle, generally unpremeditated, and nonpartisan. On one major political issue—American involvement in

Vietnam—the bias was imperceptible at first.[35] Only toward the end of the war did the networks begin to exhibit an unambiguous point of view.[36] (As late as 1968 there was virtually no relationship whatever between an individual's reliance on television and his or her opinions about Vietnam.[37]) But the non-political or nonpartisan biases which are there—those which emerge as unpremeditated organizational by-products—are real and impacting. They are the ones which count.

The beneficiary of these biases is much more likely to be a George Wallace than an Edmund Muskie or even a Ted Kennedy, despite the wishes of the individuals who produce the news.[38] And in the end, as presently constituted, the images of television news seemingly do more to decrease our own sense of self-esteem and sense of political commitment than they do to liberalize our thoughts on inflation, pollution, shortages or housing issues—which the networks routinely address but rarely influence.

The TV Audience and the News: A Strange Mix

I have suggested that the messages provided by television news are in part responsible for some portion of our political dysphoria. I have also said that the audience which the commercial networks attract to their news programs is unusually important in understanding the effects of public affairs television. But in reality the two dimensions—the unique audience and the unique content—do not merely add together to create these effects; instead they serve to multiply each other.

The Inadvertent Audience, which slides into television information, is held tightly by the information it receives. Most viewers stay tuned; most viewers watch each item, early and late, with similar intensity.[39] The news program is prepared in such a way that the Inadvertent Audience will cling to it—or, at the very least, will not turn it off. In other words, we have an unholy relationship in which the networks create images which have theatrical appeal—enervating images by which those who are very likely to be unconcerned with political information receive the information. These viewers stay with the images and are, so to speak, subliminally affected; and they are affected largely because they are politically naive. This would appear to be the best interpretation of the correlation between television dependency and political estrangement that I have found during the last several years. However, in considering our findings and our notion of an explosive interaction between audience and content, there is one other interpretation which merits consideration.

I have heard time and again that the effects I have tried to document are pseudo-effects. Generally, this refutation is based on one premise: television journalism does not cause malcontentment; it attracts it.

Under this interpretation, relying upon television for information is but the consequence of the viewer's abnormality. But although this interpretation is a responsible one, I find it unconvincing in two respects. First, one who subscribes to this interpretation is almost forced to conclude that the two-thirds of the population which has come to depend upon television news is abnormal. (It would seem difficult to argue that two-thirds of the population is abnormal, although one could make a case.) But even if we accept the premise we are still left to explain the changing level in political frustration and distrust. If television attracted only the disaffected and did not produce disaffection itself, those who doubted our institutions before the coming of the television news system would doubt them now, and we would still need to explain the growth of disaffection.

TABLE 5

Confidence in local, state, and federal government today
compared to 5 years ago*

	More confidence %	Less confidence %	About the same %	Not sure %
Local government total public	13	30	50	7
State government total public	14	26	53	7
Federal government total public	11	57	28	4

Taken from Confidence and Concern, *Louis Harris, 1973, op. cit., pp. 42-43.*

To explain that growth, one might well combine these two seemingly discrepant interpretations concerning cause and effect, blend them, and accept the final premise that television journalism has activated a latent predisposition toward political disaffection that would not, under another media system, have been so acutely or so pandemically activated.

I suspect that television journalism attracts all kinds of viewers, that one can find every intellectual, social or psychological denomination among the Advertent and Inadvertent Audiences. Among those two audiences are, to be sure, the potentially malcontent and the potentially cynical. But I still maintain that television provides the images and themes which permit those predispositions to flourish.

In the United States we have our own special political culture, a culture in which cops and politicans are either all good or all bad, depending upon the circumstance. Never having resolved too well our philosophical contradictions concerning freedom and authority, the American potential for political frustration is enormous. Thus, once television irritates those pre-disposed toward malaise, they can in turn be expected to affect (a staunch conservative would say "infect," a liberal would choose "educate") the remainder of the population, whether or not the remainder is directly sensitive to television effects. Interestingly enough, the early sixties show the greatest difference in disaffection between those relying on television and those who do not—which is to say that the differences grow smaller as the estrangement becomes severe. So those sophisticated enough to re-process the end-product of television journalism have apparently been catching up with the inadvertently informed, as the polls and the media document the growing sense of disaffection.

Again, it is not just the content which produces these effects and not just the audience, it is the mix. And to those who work to preserve the viability of the system—whatever their motives—the mix seems to serve the interest of the inadvertent viewer and the national networks more than the interest of the public at large. From this perspective the mix certainly helps explain the nearly unabated increase in hostility toward the networks by the government, regardless of the party or individuals in charge, during the last twenty years. (The Nixon years were extraordinary by any standards, however.)

The struggle between the government and the television networks deserves our attention, and the last section of the essay will treat the issue directly and at length. For now, I move to the third basic aspect of the television news system—the television network news personnel and their characteristics —which provides insight into the impact of that news system.

Television News Personnel

TV networks have neither radicals nor reactionaries in their employ. Those who might have radical or reactionary inclinations leave them at home. There is no network conspiracy to undermine the American social, economic or political system. But individual network employees possess personal character-istics and predispositions which have some effect on the political ethos in which our government operates.

I have already outlined the four-part basic equation which motivates the networks—costs, ratings, the affiliates, and the FCC. I have suggested the by-products of these motives and calculations at the organizational level. Obviously, some of the motivations of the organization filter down to the individuals—the producers, the directors, the journalists themselves. But in this discussion we focus on the more personal needs and dimensions of the network personnel—especially the correspondents.

Unfortunately, we do not know a great deal about these individuals. At the network level Edward Epstein has done the most systematic work so far, focusing on the personnel at NBC in New York.[40] There are a few other studies dealing with the people at the networks and local affiliates, and a growing number of personal interviews with, or accounts by, some of the more famous of the television news people.[41] But in fact most of our knowledge of TV newspeople is as anecdotal and impressionistic as the reports the journalists provide. Nonetheless, there are some general tendencies worth noting.

Network journalism has moved through two generations and is working through a third. The first generation was almost frivolous. John Cameron Swayze has returned to commercial advertising, from whence he came. The very notion that NBC News would ever again accept the name *The Camel News Caravan* is patently absurd. The second generation of network newspeople began in 1956 with the beginning of the Huntley-Brinkley *Report* on NBC. When Walter Cronkite replaced Douglas Edwards at CBS, the second generation had come of age. The television journalist in this period was, as a rule, a former wire services pressman, one without terribly impressive credentials—at least by today's inflated standards. Among the three patriarchs of second-generation television news—Huntley, Brinkley and Cronkite—only one, Chet Huntley, graduated from college. None of the three founding fathers attended schools of overriding prestige.

Since 1964, the year television journalism was given its press commission—the year in which the newspaper and wire services asked that the networks help them report the election returns through News Election Service—network journalism has established a new genre. The patriarchal replacements and heirs-apparent bring with them more impressive social and educational credentials than their forebears. Roger Mudd and Dan Rather both hold college degrees and both have done post-graduate work. Tom Brokaw and Garrick Utley, the men who work directly behind John Chancellor, both have degrees; Chancellor does not. Even allowing for the inflation of credentials since World War II, when one speaks about the Brahmins and near-Brahmins of television journalism, 1975, one must acknowledge the substantial upgrading that has taken place during the last ten years.

At the next level within the TV news corps the same holds true. If one lists the correspondents by age, one finds that those between thirty and fifty are generally more impressive—at least on paper—than those who are older.

Stiffening the educational prerequisites for the newer generation of television news personnel is, of course, understandable and, to most of us, commendable. But once again an ostensibly harmless alteration—an upgrading of educational prerequisites—has an important consequence.

During the last four years three sociologists, William Bowman, John Johnstone and Edward Slawski, have thoroughly investigated the factors which lead to a more activist—"participant" is their word—orientation among newspeople. They have found that, among all factors, educational experience, both in duration and quality, is the best predictor of "participant orientation."[42]

Translated, this means simply that those who have had more schooling and who have gone to "better" schools come to journalism with a more activist and aggressive set of attitudes about journalism—the "New Journalism." Given the significant differences in schooling between this generation of television news personnel and the last, one can only expect that the new news people will be more aggressive and active than their predecessors, simply as a function of their training.

There is a second factor at work here. Over and above the trend toward better schooling there is an inconspicuous trend toward a younger network corps. The expansion of the networks over the last few years has produced a corps which is, on the average, younger than that which came before. And, according to Bowman, Slawski and Johnstone, "youth" is a principal cause of participant orientation in journalism. So, as a matter of chronology, the networks have, since 1963, offered a younger staff of newspeople and presumably, as a consequence, a tougher, more aggressive one.[43] As the growth of network news staff subsides, this process will be reversed. But in this essay, at any rate, we are trying to explain the last ten years, not the next.

All told, the age factor and the "school" factor do help explain the intra-medium difference between the new and old TV news corps. The same two factors may help explain the differences between the network corps and the press corps. The factors which make the new TV newsperson a little tougher than the old also tend to make the electronic news corps a little tougher than the prominent members of the local and established press corps. But one could make too much of differences. All journalists must strain to find good copy, to get a scoop, even under circumstances that do not warrant special treatment or exciting prose. But beyond that, television newspeople seem to offer news that, compared with other local or prestige newspapers, is more disestablishmentarian. Part of the explanation may be age and schooling. But one could make too much of that, too. However, if there are differences, then at least some of it may be attributable to the status of the network newspeople and their personal styles.

Television journalism has always provided status. Until the early sixties, however, that status was awarded by the public, not by peers of the profession. But Huntley, Brinkley and Cronkite brought professional stature, as well as notoriety. A serious student of journalism could consider television as a viable alternative to a career in print. Added to that new status was the extra incentive to avoid the sullying aspects of business, law, and government. (Government became especially sullying after the beginning of the war in Vietnam.) By joining the networks one could enjoy much of the old advantages of pressmanship—independence, freedom from routine, intellectual honesty—and also enjoy all the extra advantages of television—salaries, public notoriety and an indirect involvement in national politics, involvement that was publicly acknowledged. These advantages made network journalism an honorable and incredibly desirable profession. A quick check shows that the overwhelming majority of recent occupational transfers are from print to television, not vice versa. Even when we consider the *New York Times* or the *Washington Post,* the flow is toward, not away from, the networks (Fred Graham and Sally Quinn, for example). In short, television journalism draws from among the finest young journalistic talent around—journalists who possess background and experience which are generally associated with the anti-establishment, cynical proclivities that have become the hallmark of the New Journalism. And with respect to the values of the "New Journalist," it is interesting that two of the most common political themes—and stories?—running through the minds of the network correspondents are, according to Epstein, the universal venality of politicians and the universal political disposition to seek votes instead of facing issues.[44]

So the networks may choose from the cream. And the ability to choose from the cream means, in this era, choosing from among those who are oriented toward activist journalism and cynicism.

Recalling Walter Cronkite's discussion of the television newsperson, it is interesting to note that Cronkite actually tried to disclaim a propensity for leftist politics among the network corps by admitting to a general tendency toward disestablishmentarianism.

> *As far as the leftist thing is concerned, that I think is something that comes from the nature of a journalist's work. Most newsmen have spent some time covering the seamier side of human endeavor; they cover police stations and courts and the infighting in politics.* And I think they come to feel very little allegiance to the established order. I think they're inclined to side with humanity rather than with authority and institutions. *And this sort of pushes them to the left. But I don't think there are many who are far left. I think a little left of center probably is correct.*[45] *(Emphasis is mine.)*

These cynical predispositions slip over into the news more easily than do the partisan, and with greater effect, I would surmise.

Finally, because network television has the capacity to attract virtually anyone, it has the opportunity to choose not only those who are intelligent and diligent, but those who will "fit." "Fit," of course, is hard to define; but it usually implies the ability to read copy, as well as write it, to look good, to have style. Sometimes "fit" is just a journalistic misfortune.

Recently I had the opportunity to speak with a program director for the NBC *Today* program in Washington. I asked if a decision had been reached about a replacement for Frank McGee. When I learned the matter was still unresolved, I asked if Edwin Newman had any chance whatever. Newman, in my opinion, is one of the best—well-trained, hard-working, articulate. I was told that Newman had, in fact, been considered and that he was held in highest esteem back at headquarters. But it was decided that he was "too good, too far above the audience—a liability in terms of ratings." No Newman this time around. Television is, after all, still television. But the pursuit and the prerequisite of "fit" have more serious implications than the Newman case suggests. The networks are looking for a theatrical quality, combined with journalistic skill. But theatre is still theatre. So the new journalists reflect the high-styled, high-toned, often egotistical pattern of behavior of the stage. In this, the news personnel add one more dimension to the news—self-assured, often sarcastic showmanship, a bizarre combination of Cambridge and Los Angeles. We get journalism that is young, urbane, chic, even if it is not literally Eastern-Establishment-liberal. (I suspect the revulsion for Nixon among TV reporters was rooted in style more than in conviction. It is well remembered that, before network journalists became "stylish," Nixon preferred them to print people.)

All this is not to defame the new generations of network correspondents and news personnel. They are good journalists in theory and practice, but they are also good, fashionable performers. They are becoming better and more fashionable as time goes by. A professorial-looking Paul Duke or a professorially-attired Bill Monroe are not drummed out of the business. But not too many more of their type have been invited into the TV corps. Performing has its own inevitable by-products; in this case the by-products are more cynicism, sarcasm, arrogance, sometimes hostility. And unlike print journalism, television journalism offers its nuances within the news reports. This is virtually inevitable in an audio-visual medium. The nuances blend subtly with the thematic reports that are the essence of television news. So we have an explosive concoction: thematic reports, most of which depict politics negatively, and forceful presentation, based upon theatrical skills which are themselves prone toward snippiness, if not pique. And, if Dan Rather is the archetypical case, he is certainly not the only one of his type. ABC and NBC have tried—and some say they have tried desperately hard—to emulate the Rather model by recruiting and quickly promoting Tom Jarriel and Tom Brokaw.

In summary, it appears that the very qualities which make up the contemporary network correspondent—youth, big-city life, a moderately prestigious background, theatrical skills—are the qualities which lead first of all to a pronounced affinity for activist journalism and secondly to a "modish" disaffection from conventional society and conventional politics. It would also appear that style, pique and hostility are keys to both success and effectiveness in network reporting. In any event, the combination of organizational needs of the network and the general make-up of the news staffs produce images which are most assuredly negative and are also very probably effective. Daniel Moynihan may have been wrong in assuming that the press corps is a frustrated elite. But he was probably right in implying that those who count in the press corps—which clearly implies the network press corps—act as if they were.[46]

What's more, the effectiveness of the network reporter is apparently enhanced by the high credibility of the journalists and the networks (popularity is a better term),[47] the comparative lack of control editors and producers can exert over their correspondents,[48] and the parasocial interaction which occurs between the journalist and his fans.[49] So we have an unconscious network news formula, based on impressions of politics and society and patterned upon the professional values and the personal styles of the most popular news people. This formula has been at the heart of television journalism for quite some time, long before the Watergate break-in or the advent of the war in Vietnam.

But one can carry on these criticisms too long. Given the unique demands and limitations placed upon them, the people of television journalism do a good job at much of what they do. It is not surprising, for example, that through network television the nation has appreciably increased its general awareness of politics, issues and politicians. But, given the unique demands and limitations placed upon them, it should not be surprising that the people of television journalism have also helped to produce a more disaffected, alienated and frustrated electorate.

The News as a Source of Political Indoctrination

Every society must teach itself and its young that its basic values are good and its institutions are appropriate for achieving those values. In other words, each society, pluralistic or monolithic, must peddle legitimacy. It is this belief in and commitment to the values and institutions—it is legitimacy—that allows a nation to transcend brief crises or endure prolonged periods of deprivation. Consequently, every nation must teach, train, socialize and indoctrinate its own by conditioning them to believe. Authoritarian regimes seize control, directly or indirectly, of all the major sectors of society which can contribute to attitudes which are conducive to social sacrifice, patriotism, commitment. The sectors most important in socializing individuals are the family, the peers, the schools, the private social organizations, the government and the media. An anti-democratic regime wants to control them all and compel each to trumpet the same basic supportive themes. A democratic regime is less committed to control and, by choice, places the governmental sector at odds with itself—calling part the government and the remainder the opposition. This division, presumably, serves several societal interests, among them the preservation of individual liberty, which is preserved, hopefully, through a disunified and changing political authority. But to achieve one social value—liberty—implies sacrificing another—commitment to the regime. Democratic regimes consider the trade-off worthwhile—less indoctrination, more liberty.

Democratic regimes also permit a greater degree of freedom for their media, usually extending much greater freedom to the press than to electronic media. Again, this is done to ensure the preservation of one or more basic values—in this case the preferred values being truth, liberty, freedom of thought and the promotion of honesty in public or private life. But, once again, to achieve these values—to remove the media from direct political control—makes the basic process of political inculcation more difficult. And the more expansive the system of media, the more difficult the process. This relationship best explains the almost universal tendency for governments to refuse to allow television independence from political authority, even if the press is free. In this respect, American television is *sui generis,* being by far the most independent of all television systems on earth.

Before the development of modern television journalism in the United States, among the agencies which were responsible for fostering our basic political beliefs, there were four which had direct contact with the individual and which, in general, tended to support the political leaders of the moment, as well as the political system: family, peers, secondary social organizations, and the party controlling the government. With the exception of a miniscule intelligentsia, only the political opposition, working through the media, provided information which was appreciably declamatory. Only the opposition, working through the media, said that the nation was falling apart, moving backward, losing its purity or its way. But the opposition was always expected to provide this information. In that capacity the opposition had little credibility. Until television journalism changed this delicate balance, there was only one opposition at any one time. The President was, at that point, the strongest, most capable, hardest-working person in the entire world, to almost every American child.[50]

This balance has come unstuck. The network news organizations have become, in concert, a highly credible, never-tiring political opposition, a maverick third party which never need face the sobering experience of governing. Newspapers, to some extent, might long ago have achieved this same status; in fact they did, to a limited degree. But newspapers are faceless; they have no visible spokesmen. Their information is less vibrant and most often ignored by the bulk of the electorate. We must not forget that the vast majority of our citizens never read the newspapers, they glanced at them. It has always been the political sophisticate—the one less likely to succumb to media malaise from the start—who moves past page one.

If one accepts this behavioristic interpretation of political legitimacy which I am offering, one can regard television as a new and more compelling political opposition—an opposition which, by its political messages, causes the conditioned linkage between the public and the regime to grow less strong, less invincible. This would be especially true in the portions of the population which display a less sophisticated, less well-thought-out commitment to the society. Significantly, as we have seen, this happens to be the same segment of the population which receives the greatest amount of and exhibits the greatest dependence upon television journalism.

To state the theory more directly, television journalism has altered the long-established balance between *patriating* agencies—segments of society which generally portray our condition as favorable and preferable—and *dispatriating* agencies—those which generally portray our condition as wretched or becoming more so. One might say that even without the "New Journalism," the decline in belief in our institutions and ourselves was inevitable, given the change in ratio between patriating and dispatriating sources of information.

One might also say that this process is inexorable in a system which maintains a wholly free and competitive journalism. One might formulate another series of dismal laws: (1) As the amount of information from a free, competitive media increases, the ratio of patriating to dispatriating information decreases. (2) As the ratio of patriating to dispatriating information decreases, belief and support for political institutions decrease as well. In other words, the more information the population receives, the more politically estranged the population becomes, especially among that segment which has been given only a civics-book exposure to American politics.

While these laws may seem as bleak as they do reductionist, it is not terribly difficult to accept them, given the pattern of public opinion in the United States, especially since 1963, the year in which dispatriating information increased substantially on the heels of the 30-minute news format. (There was, perhaps, a much greater increase in "dispatriating" information than suggested by doubling the length of the news. The 15-minute program was perhaps 10 minutes of straight AP reportage with little vividly dispatriating information—5 minutes at most. The 30-minute telecast contains the same 10 minutes of wire and 20 minutes of thematic information—potentially dispatriating information.)

There is one final point about the ratio of patriating and dispatriating information. If we accept the general behavioristic model, we might consider the specific ramifications of a shift in the ratio. In concrete terms, let us imagine that if all sources of opinion were controlled by the government the average citizen would feel 99 percent sure that his society and its political process were legitimate. But in pursuit of liberty we add an opposition party, a party which claims that things are bad and bound to get worse, etc. We find the same hypothetical citizen is now only 95 percent certain about his political system. Add free media and the change will not be 4 percent but, perhaps, as great as 8 percent. Add commercial, uncontrolled television to the system, and for our hypothetical citizen the loss may be, on the average, another 16 points. This is the general pattern that exists in psychological research when one changes the ratio of conditioning and extinguishing situations.[51] One discovers a geometric increase or decrease in conditioned response.

For those of you who find both this set of suppositions about public opinion and the analogy to Pavlovian psychology callous or without merit, I suggest that you reconsider before dismissing either premise. Virtually every authoritarian regime operates under these very suppositions, and so does every democratic regime, excluding, to some degree, the United States. After all, all of the western democracies except the United States allow newspapers to publish freely but stringently regulate or directly control their television networks.

Of course *neither the networks nor the opposition in the United States are unpatriotic because they are dispatriating!* The relationship between patriotism and patriationism is terribly difficult to sort out. I trust it is an insoluble problem. But, in any event, the networks, like the opposition, *are* dispatriating influences. And given our own sensitivity to any decrease in affection for our political institutions, even the relatively low level and watered-down quality of the dispatriating information offered by the opposition and the networks has had dramatic repercussions. And, of course, there have been decreases in our sense of self-confidence and our sense of institutional pride during the last decade. But before blowing the whistle on our dispatriating networks or our dispatriating opposition merely because they can dispatriate, we should put all our findings and all our interpretations into an empirical as well as a normative perspective.

Costs and Benefits of Television Journalism: Some Observations

Somehow, whenever I offer my opinions about television to students, journalists or colleagues, the ghost of Spiro T. Agnew seems to waft into the room. Frankly, I would like to have his ghost thrown out once and for all. I do not offer these thoughts with Agnewian vituperation or with an Agnewian sense of ulterior motive. I do believe, however, that there are serious issues to be raised concerning our most conspicuous medium.

Free media, just like free elections, represent a trade-off for any society—a trade-off from which is derived some "good" at the price of some "evil." On balance, I do not argue against free elections or a free press, or free television, for that matter. I suggest only that free television journalism has produced some effects which are socially "functional" and some which are "dysfunctional" (dysfunctional being the ultimate euphemism for that which is not supportive of the on-going regime) and that these effects must be considered together. In short, television journalism, like all free journalism, provides a classic case in cost-benefit analysis. On the plus side we get (1) a more widely-informed electorate; (2) a purer political process; and (3) a more responsive set of political institutions.

Television journalism has unquestionably increased the aggregate level of political information, i.e., politically relevant facts, although information itself can sometimes be a cost. For example, a strong case can be made that without network television neither George McGovern nor Eugene McCarthy could have gained nearly enough political notoriety to pull their respective coups in the 1968 and 1972 Democratic primaries. (These two cases suggest both the power of television to make people aware of something as well as the difficulty one experiences in trying to decide if more information is always a benefit.)

Network journalism has also discouraged venality and corruption in those areas where television has been permitted to go and has wished to go. The national nominating convention is the prime example. There can be little question that the chair and the delegates behave more fairly and seriously than they did before the arrival of television. The enormous range of network journalism has triggered a new morality in political life. Watergate indiscretions notwithstanding, network television has made *overt* corruption in the White House, for instance, a contemporary impossibility.

The purity which television journalism brings is not itself directly relevant to policy. But there are implications for policy to be found here. The same process which produces institutional purity produces institutional responsiveness as well. In essence, network journalism makes the law of anticipated reaction much more binding on those individuals and institutions which receive coverage. Politicians and bureaucrats are virtually terrified of exposure by the networks. So strong is that terror that if one can make a patently legitimate case about some political (or economic) injustice through the networks, he or she can count on winning the case. In other words, the networks can compel responsiveness from bureaucrats or corporate executives, if conditions are right.

During the spring of 1974 thousands of the veterans who were eligible for education benefits and who were not receiving them—6% of those eligible—sought redress from the Veterans Administration. This was an injustice, and a blatant one in terms of our national feelings about war veterans. The *New York Times* and the *Washington Post* had covered this story intermittently since the previous autumn, when the academic year began. But there had been little, if any, noticeable effect. Immediately following an exposé on the NBC *Nightly News*—an exposé based upon a lengthy story in the *Post*, it would appear—the President contacted the VA, demanded a quick response, and eventually requested that VA Director Johnson be retired.

This is just one instance in which the networks, by picking up a story from the larger, more investigative newspapers, stimulate a quick and decent response from the institution or individual having administrative jurisdiction. But there is another side to the ledger. Television journalism, unfettered and acting in a way which serves its organizational interests, does not always serve the public interest—whether one believes that the regime is blemishless or merely worth saving.

Television journalism can undermine our trust in our fellow man, increase racial hostility, and exacerbate the anti-democratic strain which has historically run through our culture.[52] But more relevant to us is the effect of television on our sense of legitimacy. This is, however, a more difficult issue to handle. Television may very well be undermining our national sense of legitimacy. But if one should accept the validity of that premise, one still faces a different but equally important issue: is our growing illegitimacy justified? Is this illegitimacy really a negative development? Is our growing illegitimacy, in a word, legitimate?

Before addressing these questions, I offer two essential caveats: (1) that our crisis in legitimacy may be imaginary, and (2) that given a strictly behavioristic interpretation of legitimacy it is impossible to consider issues such as these.

The Crisis in Legitimacy: Strange as this may seem, I am not wholly convinced that we have a crisis in legitimacy. Part of the "crisis" is undoubtedly a mirage based on the survey items we use to measure change in attitude. While two out of three Americans may now believe that their government is untrustworthy, the vast majority still believes the basic governmental structure is worth saving and worth fighting for. Surveyors don't ask these questions too often, because the answers stay pretty much the same through time and surveyors want items that will demonstrate change—items that will justify continuing the surveys. One might argue that the "crisis" exists using only certain measures, or, on the other hand, that the crisis may be great in comparative terms but slight in absolute terms. In short, our notion that we are in a state of crisis may be an invalid one given us by our mass media, which love to reveal discomfiture, and our pollsters, who love to demonstrate change.

There is a second point which a commitment to intellectual honesty compels me to raise. Before discussing the legitimacy of growing illegitimacy, I must hedge on my behavioristic theory of legitimacy. If the level of legitimacy is, as I have argued, merely determined by the ratio of patriating to dispatriating sources of information, it is foolishness to speak about a justifiable level of support for the political system. The level of support is given, and that is that. But I cannot be so crassly deterministic. I believe that there is a grey area in interpreting legitimacy, one in which legitimacy is neither a totally behavioristic quotient nor a wholly evidential assessment of the system. In fact, I believe that, despite the caveats mentioned here, there *is* at least some erosion of political legitimacy in our society and that we can meaningfully discuss whether or not this erosion is justifiable, despite the generally behavioristic definition of legitimacy that has been posited.

As do most political scientists under thirty, I tend to believe that our growing illegitimacy is deserved. The American people have been, perhaps, too enamored with their political institutions for too long. The public has either ignored or remained unaware of serious contradictions and malfeasance within the political process. The public has been overly sanguine about our politics and our politicians. In this respect, the decline in legitimacy which television has fostered is justified.

But even if the general decline is defendable, the role which television has played in this affair has not been without blemish. The erosion in public trust and public confidence has been more the product of the imperatives of Madison Avenue than of an innocent pursuit of truth. And consequently the erosion in legitimacy has been relatively perverse, with the public rightly questioning their institutions but for the wrong reasons and in the wrong way. Specifically, the public has come to believe that things are worse than they *were*—that all this misery and misfortune is *new* to America and the world. The images of television have somehow persuaded the public that the society is coming apart, moving downward from where it once was. And this persuasion is as demonstrable as it is bizarre. As late as November, 1973, fifteen times as many adult Americans believed they as individuals were "doing well" as believed the country was doing well![53] In short, television's images are imbalanced and distorted. The effects of these images are distorted too, almost perversely. In that context, the impact of television on political perception is unjustified or, at least, criticisable.

Of course the networks are not responsible for most of the events which have been a necessary condition in our malaise. The networks did not invent the break-in at Watergate, inflate the dollar, authorize illegal bombings, arrange political assassinations, etc. Nor do the networks lie, although they've been known to cheat a little.[54]

But the networks speak to an audience which contains an enormous pool of politically unskilled individuals—those who rely on an eighth-grade civics curriculum to comprehend national politics. Their perceptions are not only limited, they are also naive. Television's focus is murderous for these people. It is in no way surprising that I have found that reliance upon television journalism is associated with greater support for George Wallace, especially among middle-status Americans.[55] These are the individuals who shifted first toward political cynicism and frustration, moving others along in time. And I suspect that the revelations about Watergate have hit this group particularly hard. These revelations will also, I suspect, tend to unleash the networks and compel them to provide even more of those images of society which so totally overwhelm middle-America. We may, in fact, be on the verge of a new era of television malaise, one that will begin now that impeachment and the fate of Richard Nixon have been resolved.

Recommendations

Given my criticisms of the networks, I feel obligated to say something about reform. Unfortunately, there is little to say. If one wishes to diminish the "dysfunctional" effects which television has brought with it, one faces a virtually insoluble dilemma: most of the changes that would work would be either antilibertarian, unconstitutional or unacceptable to the networks. We can never even consider limiting the audience; that would be patently unconstitutional. We cannot change the content very much without violating the Fairness Doctrine. We cannot expect networks to limit their coverage of Washington; that would be both antilibertarian and economically infeasible. In short, there is little to recommend that seems both plausible and meaningful. Nevertheless, I shall suggest three things which might render the networks less unsettling and would clearly render them less vulnerable to criticism.

One of the most conspicuous characteristics of television journalism is its search for the individual case which demonstrates some lesson, generally a lesson involving some social or political snafu. Given the need for thematic reports, this is a wholly understandable phenomenon. News executives believe that when a correspondent needs to examine the impact of public policy, the correspondent should find a case and film it. Unfortunately, when the networks follow the effects of policy in this way they are engaging in an especially "unfair" practice, one which I shall call the dilemma of the Lady-or-the-Tiger technique.

Imagine a hypothetical case. The networks do a film piece on a federally-sponsored welfare program in Chicago. The journalist points out that budgetary cuts have jeopardized this particular program, despite reasonable protest by the local black community. The implication is usually clear. When a community lacks middle-class credentials, there is nothing that anybody can do. The citizens are victims of their condition. They have no money, no skills, no status, no college training to parlay into political clout. The government fails the unfortunate.

Now imagine a governmental decision that has implications for our group in Chicago. Imagine that the government cuts defense spending and spending in related areas and increases HEW allotments for social services. What can we expect from the networks? We should not expect a piece on the program in Chicago which has managed to survive. Instead we should expect a feature about shipbuilders in Rhode Island who have been laid-off, who are victims of a government policy that has taken away their bread and butter. Once again, to accommodate, the government increases its appropriations for the Navy and decides to cut funds for developing supersonic aircraft. Now we can expect to find the networks in Seattle interviewing an aeronautical engineer whose future is jeopardized by the decision to stop funding for the SST. This time the implication is different. The government is not responsive to college-educated, skilled professionals. The government fails those who have worked hard and played by the rules.

Of course in some respects this story is contrived. The government is not quite so flexible; these events would take years, not months to transpire. But the cases are not hypothetical; I have seen them all, almost as a package. I do not doubt that each story is a true one, but I object to the method of presentation, which is without proper context and which, for the viewer, must certainly be an undeclared choice between the lady and the tiger. To cut defense spending directly implies unemployment at navy yards or air bases or somewhere. To decide to help the poor, low-status and unskilled because they are poor, low-status and unskilled is a fine goal for public policy. In the real world of budgeting, however, such a decision means that you would be giving less help to those who are not poor, not low-status, not unskilled.

If the networks must cover these types of cases in the human condition—and I, for one, think they should—they have a responsibility to put them into a meaningful context by making clear that unemployment in Seattle is the necessary, if sorry, outcome of deciding against the SST. But the networks generally do not place these types of stories in context; at best they append the edited and too-brief comments of an "opposing spokesman," who also serves as adversary and neglects to make plain the dilemmas of public policy.

By following this technique—by showing the negative consequences of policy A or policy not-A—the networks are not only promoting a perception of government policy that is unjustifiably dismal (especially when this particular theme is combined with the theme of "the good old days"), they are also behaving at least somewhat irresponsibly. If one must decry Seattle, one must "explain" Seattle and consider the difficulty in trying to achieve unspecified ends with specific policies. If there is a dilemma, point it out. It would probably be worth the added public confusion to educate viewers in the cruel world of economic and social trade-offs. The first recommendation must be to insist that studies dealing with the effects of government policy be treated more sophisticatedly and less dramatically, with greater appreciation of costs and benefits.

The second recommendation is more concrete than the first. I suggest that the networks make a concerted effort to include more stories based upon systematic and quantitative research, research that individuals or organizations outside the networks have conducted.

Ironically, with the exception of Dow Jones and a few statistics from the Department of Labor, the only systematic research that works its way regularly into the CBS News, generally regarded as the best of the three, is a four-city study in which food prices are checked month by month. The journalist in New York, Los Angeles, Chicago or Atlanta returns to the same store each month to buy the same items he or she bought the month before.

Each shopper then displays his or her findings about the cost of a basket of food which in mid-1973 was exactly twenty dollars. I would guess that this on-going research was adopted when the news department was virtually convinced that prices would go up enough each month to justify this research as "news." (It will be interesting to see what CBS does should retail food prices ever stabilize. My intuition tells me that only inflationary increases can justify both the story as news and the cost of continuing the research.) In a word, systematic research is not the forte or even the concern of the networks.

But there is a need for and, I think, an obligation to include more stories which are not anecdotal or impressionistic, stories based in social science research. A five- or ten-minute segment given over to the social or financial or even the physical sciences would serve a necessary end. And once again, even if this suggested technique does not affect the ratings or the impact of the news, it will still increase the stature of the network news organizations and render them a more serious journalistic enterprise.

In 1972, CBS, seeking perhaps to enhance its own professional stature, attempted to do something similar to that which I have recommended. They offered on the evening news a lengthy (20-minute) evidential and sophisticated treatment of the large American wheat sale to the Soviet Union. Pleased with itself, CBS attempted a second feature, this time on Watergate. Due to political pressure the second feature was the last. But the shortcoming of this technique was a political one.[56] In general, I think that the addition of a research segment is well within the realm of the plausible, even given the realities of commercial television.

Finally, I think that there is a compelling need for the networks to reconsider the criteria used in selecting correspondents. The general trend has been toward bright, well-educated, highly-stylized reporters. But the most recent additions to the networks seem to suggest an even greater concern for style. I understand that this recommendation gets dangerously close to the heart of commercial television—that recruitment may be too fundamental an issue even to be seriously discussed by the laity, given the economic and political ground rules under which the networks operate. Nonetheless, I suggest that the networks might choose new correspondents who are no less energetic or hard-working but who are less adversarial and less hostile than some the networks have recently chosen. Zealousness is not new to American journalism, nor is zealousness necessarily a vice. But it would seem that the networks have shifted recently from essentially press people to essentially television people. This is, from my perspective, an unfortunate development, and I would prefer that the networks return to the newspaper people and move away from the recent genre, one in which the local affiliates have become the farm teams for network correspondents.

I should point out that these recommendations are not necessarily going to alter the effects attributed to network journalism. But these recommendations will make the networks look better and decrease their vulnerability to attack—attacks which would be far less sympathetic than mine or even those which have sprung up recently in *TV Guide.*

Even so I am a realist. I recognize that the networks are sensitive to criticism and reluctant to change. They argue that my theory is either wrong—factually inaccurate—or that it is irrelevant to them because they are only reporting what goes on. One network producer suggested that my theory was correct once but that since Watergate, and especially since the network coverage of the House Judiciary hearings on impeachment, my theory has become "obsolete," that network journalism has increased our national sense of legitimacy. Perhaps so. But I gain the distinct impression that the networks may grow more the way they have been, almost as a consequence of their commendable role in the Watergate crisis. At any rate, I suspect that network journalism will continue to grow and that the public will become continually more dependent upon it. Under these circumstances, the theory of Videomalaise will, I fear, no longer be obsolete, inaccurate or irrelevant to any of us.

Finally, despite all my criticisms and anxieties I must conclude that, on balance, to this point the network system has been beneficial, perhaps more beneficial than the older system of communication. Of course, regardless of the beneficial balance there is little that we can do with our news system, one way or the other. Our present system will not be altered by the government; that would be politically unrealistic. Nor will the system be changed by the networks; that would be economically unrealistic. We are, so to speak, stuck with the potential and partially-realized effects. Until we, as a people, grow more sophisticated in understanding our own governmental process and our own communications process, these effects will not abate. So if reform seems so remote, one might ask, what's the point of all these interpretations and prescriptions?

The point is this: Americans consensually believe that despite its costs democracy is the best form of government. We also believe that despite its costs a free market is the best form of economy. And, as Americans, we have never doubted that a free press is the best form of communication. Network television has merely underscored the necessity to add, once again, that terribly important phrase: despite its costs. In the shadow of Vietnam and Watergate we sometimes forget.

Footnotes

1.   *For a thorough and interesting empirical test of this premise, see S.M. Lipset,* Political Man: The Social Bases of Politics *(Garden City, New York: Anchor, 1963), chapter 3.*

2.   Confidence and Concern: Citizens View American Government, *U.S. Government Printing Office, 1973, p. 33.*

3.   *Cited in* Washington Post, *January 8, 1974, p. 2.*

4.   *Arthur Miller, Thad Brown, Alden Raine, "Social Conflict and Political Estrangement, 1958-72," paper presented at Midwest Political Science Association Convention, May, 1973, pp. 7-13.*

5.   *There is some evidence that between 1968 and 1970 the decline in public trust and discontent abated. See Arthur Miller, "Political Issues and Trust in Government," paper presented at the American Political Science Association, September, 1972, also found in* The American Political Science Review, *Vol. 68, September, 1974, pp. 951-972.*

6.   Ibid., *p. 2.*

7.   *Michael Robinson, "Public Affairs Television and the Growth of Political Malaise: The Case of the Selling of the Pentagon," unpublished, Ph.D. dissertation, University of Michigan, 1972; also forthcoming, with the same title,* American Political Science Review.

8.   *Michael Robinson, "The Impact of the Televised Watergate Hearings,"* Journal of Communication, *Vol. 24:2; Spring 74, 17-30.*

9.   Ibid., *pp. 28-29.*

10.   *Michael Robinson, "Public Affairs Television . . . ," op. cit., especially chapter 3 and conclusions.*

11.   *I use the 1968 data because they are the most recent available with questions concerning the comparative reliance on all types of mass media. Unfortunately, from our perspective, the Survey Research Center in Ann Arbor chose not to use the very questions which would have permitted a similar analysis with the 1972 national election study.*

12.   *Michael Robinson, "Public Affairs Television . . . ," op. cit., p. 185.*

13.   *Harvey Gersin, "The Dimension and Growth of Network Evening News," unpublished xerox, ABC News Research and Development, July, 1973, pp. 1-3.*

14.   Burns Roper, What People Think of Television and Other Mass Media, 1959-1972, *Television Information Office, New York, May, 1973.*

15.   *See Michael Robinson and Clifford Zukin, "Television and the Wallace Vote in 1968: Are There Implications for 1976?", paper presented at American Association of Public Opinion Research Convention, Lake George, New York, May, 1974; also in* Public Opinion Quarterly, *Vol. 38, Fall, 1974, p. 445.*

16.   *CBS News, telephone survey, March 20, 1970, reproduced in Hazel Erskine's "The Polls: Opinion of the News Media," in* Public Opinion Quarterly, *Vol. 34, Winter, 1970-71, p. 632.*

17. *John Robinson, "The Impact of Television on Mass Media Usage: A Cross-National Comparison," paper presented at 6th World Congress of Sociology, Evian, France, September, 1966, p. 2.*

18. *Robert Bower,* Television and the Public *(New York: Holt, 1973), p. 132.*

19. *Elihu Katz, "The Two-Step Flow of Communication: An Up-To-Date Report on an Hypothesis,"* Public Opinion Quarterly, *Vol. 21, Spring, 1957, pp. 61-78.*

20. *Elihu Katz and Paul Lazarsfeld,* Personal Influence: The Part Played by People in the Flow of Mass Communications *(Glencoe: The Free Press, 1955).*

21. *Although nobody has systematically demonstrated the end of the two-step flow (nobody ever really demonstrated its existence), there is literature to suggest that process is no longer what it once was. See E.M. Rogers,* The Communication of Innovations *(New York: Free Press, 1972). The Roper data on sources of information also suggest that the links between the media and the public have become very direct. Burns Roper,* What People Think., *op. cit.*

22. *John Robinson, op. cit., p. 1.*

23. *Edward Epstein,* News From Nowhere *(New York: Random House, 1973), pp. 211-212.*

24. *"Interview with Walter Cronkite: A Candid Conversation With America's Most Trusted Newsman,"* Playboy, *June, 1973, p. 76.*

25. *This study, supported by the American Enterprise Institute in Washington, is currently being completed at Ohio State University. Publication of this monumental work will occur late this year.*

26. *Michael Robinson, "Public Affairs Television . . .," op. cit., pp. 169-170.*

27. *See Note 25. Most of these data show a pattern of neutrality. But there are far more negative items than positive.*

28. *For an interesting discussion of the network news format see Paul Weaver, "Is Television News Biased?"* Public Interest, *Winter, 1972, pp. 57-74.*

29. Washington Post, *Sunday, February 17, 1974, p. A1, p. A4.*

30. *It is impossible to determine, at this point, if any of the networks did include the story. The reports in the* Post *and* Times *came out on a Sunday. I watched both NBC and CBS that evening and saw no mention of the report. I checked the Vanderbilt Index and Abstracts and found no entries whatever for Sunday, February 17, 1974.*

31.   *George Gerbner and Larry Gross, "Violence Profile 6: Trends in Network Television Drama and Viewer Conceptions of Social Reality, 1967-1973," mimeo, University of Pennsylvania, December, 1974.*

32.   *Michael J. Robinson, "Public Affairs Television . . . ," op. cit., especially chapter 3.*

33.   *Ernest Lefever,* TV and National Defense: An Analysis of CBS News 1972-1973, *(Boston, Virginia: Institute for American Strategy, 1974), chapter 2.*

34.   *Jeff Ring, "The Eastern and Urban Orientation of the National News," unpublished term paper, Eugene, Oregon, 1973, p. 11.*

35.   *This point is disputed by Efron. But there is evidence to support a theory of balanced coverage of Vietnam in the early stages. See Frank Russo, "A Study of Bias in TV Coverage of the Vietnam War: 1969-1970,"* Public Opinion Quarterly, *Vol. 35, 1972, 539-543.*

36.   *Although Lefever would probably dispute the premise that the early coverage of Vietnam was balanced, comparatively speaking, it is clear that Lefever has demonstrated that by 1972, the balance had been seriously eroded. E. Lefever,* TV and the National Defense, *op. cit., especially chapter 5.*

37.   *Michael Robinson, "Public Affairs Television . . . ," op. cit., p. 148.*

38.   *Michael Robinson, et al. "Television and the Wallace Vote . . . ," op. cit.*

39.   *Russ Neuman, "Exploring the Impact of Television News," unpublished mimeo, Berkeley, 1972.*

40.   *Edward Epstein,* News From Nowhere, *op. cit., passim, especially chapter 7.*

41.   *James Buckalew, "The Television News Editor as Gatekeeper,"* Journal of Broadcasting, *Vol. 13, No. 1, 1968-1696, 48-49; and "News Elements and Selection by Television News Editors," same journal, Winter 1969-1970, 47-53. Also see George Bailey and Lawrence Lichty, "Rough Justice on a Saigon Street,"* Journalism Quarterly, *Vol. 49, Summer, 1972, 221-238. Insiders include William Small,* To Kill a Messenger *(New York: Hastings House, 1972); Robert MacNeil (New York: Harper and Row, 1968); Fred Friendly,* Due To Circumstances Beyond Our Control *(New York: Random House, 1967).*

42.   *John Johnstone, Edward Slawski, William Bowman, "The Professional Values of American Newsmen,"* Public Opinion Quarterly, *Vol. 36, Winter, 1972-73, p. 259.*

43.   *Age is negatively correlated with a participant orientation. John Johnstone, et al, op. cit., p. 537.*

44. *Edward Epstein, op. cit., pp. 215-219.*

45. *Walter Cronkite interview, op. cit., p. 76.*

46. *Daniel P. Moynihan, "The President and the Press,"* Commentary, *March, 1971.*

47. *Oliver Quayle discovered that Cronkite is the most credible person in the nation. The Harris poll shows that television news has, in the last year, increased its credibility more than any other social agency. See note 2 for citation.*

48. *William Small,* To Kill a Messenger *(New York: Hastings House, 1970), p. 280.*

49. *Leslie Sargent, "Communicator Image and News Reception,"* Journal of Communication, *Vol. 42, 35-42.*

50. *Among others, Fred Greenstein, "The Benevolent Leader: Children's Images of Political Authority,"* American Political Science Review, *Vol. 54, 1960, 934-943.*

51. *Delos Wickens and Donald Meyer,* Psychology *(New York: Holt, 1961), chapter 3.*

52. *Michael Robinson, "Public Affairs Television . . . ," op. cit., "Conclusions."*

53. *Cited in* Time *magazine, November 19, 1973, p. 25.*

54. *Following the broadcast of* The Selling of the Pentagon *there were several charges made: that CBS had, in that documentary, done unethical editing, that CBS had earlier on incorrectly attributed a child's death to malnutrition in* Hunger in America, *and that CBS had actually paid Haitian revolutionaries so that CBS camera crews might follow clandestine operations in the Caribbean. CBS has not denied these assertions. In fact, President Salant has tacitly admitted to the last two by stating that in one case the baby's cause of death was indeterminable, and in the second, that "no significant amount" of money was involved in the Haitian incident.*

55. *Michael Robinson, et al., "Television and the Wallace Vote . . . ," op. cit.*

56. *Timothy Crouse,* The Boys on the Bus *(New York: Random House, 1973), pp. 173-175.*

I think we tend to judge TV from a point in time, and this can be misleading. TV is not now what it was or what it will be; nor are we. The point is obvious, but we tend to forget it. For example, books aren't now all hand-lettered on vellum, nor is the theater a low art form; nor is TV what it was when it started. Today we see TV quite differently than, let us say, a child of three will eventually grow up to conceive of it. What we see as a weakness now might be ignored by that child as not even an issue .... We have to be careful not to overestimate our own place in history and personal experiences in trying to understand television.

James Kraft

The Electronic Community: A New Environment for Television Viewers and Critics

Kas Kalba

Problems of pollution, crime, health and education have caused city life to deteriorate for most people . . . We have investigated ways of enabling more of the population to live in attractive rural environments and to combine that mode of life with some of the amenities offered by large cities. Employment, improved health and educational services, cultural and entertainment opportunities and so on could be provided for every part of the country through the imaginative application of telecommunications technology.

(Peter C. Goldmark, *"Communication and the Community,"* in Scientific American, *September 1972, describing the New Rural Society project.*)

> *In the wild my gazelles still stand erect*
> *when they first see me.*
> *They pinpoint me through binoculars then scamper.*
> *So does the panther, gopher, rhino, mouse.*
> *But my city animals will run and will attack me.*
> *The Xerox bites my tail.*
> *The toaster snaps at fingers.*
> *The refrigerator quivers; vacuum cleaner sucks;*
> *typewriter stings like a B.*
> *My TV set complains.*
> *And the telephone, when we are all alone,*
> *winds its cord around my neck.*

(Standing Animals, *a poem on the electronic future or present.*)

Kas Kalba is Lecturer on city planning at Harvard University's Graduate School of Design and President of Kalba Bowen Associates, Inc., communications consultants.

141

The following essay is premised on the belief that there is more (and not less) to television than meets the eye. Television, I will argue, affects not only our senses through its progamming and our pocketbooks through its commercials, but also our entire social and cultural environment. The technology of television affects, and is affected by, the culture of television, which in turn has an impact on overall social change.

More specifically, the essay represents an attempt to speculate about the future of television. The future that will be considered is not that of television alone but of related emerging technologies as well, especially those associated with cable television. For if the recent projections of both equipment manufacturers and social visionaries are accurate, the TV household of today is soon to be transformed into a supermarket of electronic gadgetry, connected to the outside world by the electronic highway of cable communications.

According to these projections, tomorrow's household will contain a facsimile copier to capture the day's news; a remote learning and shopping terminal; a videotape recorder for delayed playback of entertainment and cultural programming; special terminals to give access to computational services, bank accounts and office files; a wall-size TV screen for viewing abstract art or baseball games; monitoring systems that will prevent burglaries and heart attacks; a television camera for two-way video conferences; and a variety of other communications services and devices. The role of electronics in American life, which has already adapted to the telegraph, the telephone, the record player, and the TV set, will have been extended *ad infinitum,* and, some would add, *ad absurdum.*

As one cartoonist has already depicted, the human anatomy may have to be considerably modified merely to cope with this new technological outpouring. The eyes and ears will expand in proportion to the increased sensory input at their disposal. The hands will grow additional fingers to be able to push all the buttons. Legs will shrink and atrophy while the rump quadruples in size, since there will be little need for walking or traveling. This cynical caricature of humanity adapting to technology's needs (rather than the converse) may hold considerable truth and serve as an appropriate epitaph to our captivation by technology's unbridled progress.

Yet there is another vision of the impact that the new electronic media will have on our social and community structure. After all, the services that will become available over the home communications consoles of tomorrow may merely supplement rather than replace those that are already available today. They may do away with the inconveniences of having to write a letter in order to make a reservation or of having to watch a television program at a pre-scheduled time. They may expand our choice with respect to shopping goods, jobs, political viewpoints, and cultural or educational amenities. They may increase our access to medical and social services. And they may diminish our reliance on the automobile for personal mobility, thereby decreasing traffic congestion, air pollution, and energy consumption in a single swoop.

It is difficult to choose between these two perspectives of our communications future. One appeals to our long-standing faith in technological betterment, the other to our growing disenchantment with this belief. However, the two perspectives converge in one respect—they both foresee the emergence of a new communications environment that will alter our lives as members of families, as consumers, as citizens, and as cultural beings. And, as I will argue in the following pages, they both raise profound issues concerning the evolution of our "electronic community," issues that television critics and policy makers have hardly begun to contemplate.

Television and Community Life

If the impact of new communications technology on community life will be dramatic in the years ahead, it will not be entirely without precedent. Communications media have already affected the structure of our communities in the past, particularly in recent decades. The questions that I will pursue in the first part of this essay bear on the role of television in community life. How has television initiated or reinforced changes in family life? How has it affected social communication and urban development? By answering these questions some valuable insights can be gained into the possible future impact of communications media.

Family and Social Communication

There are several images of what members of the family used to do before television appeared in the nineteen fifties. One is that they spent a great deal of the evening hours interacting, either with each other or with relatives and neighbors. The family talked at length around the dinner table, sang songs together, or even if they listened to the radio they did so only to reinforce the intimacy of the family spirit. A second image is that the members of the family simply spent more time working before television's arrival. Long hours at the factory, long hours doing chores, or long hours cleaning house—these were the time killers. Finally, a third view suggests that the members of the family did not communicate very much, even though they had the time to do so. Off-hours were spent out on the porch peering into space, or each member pursued his or her own activities, whether needlepoint, drinking at the local bar, or reading.

Undoubtedly, each of these images is an exaggeration or applies only to some portion of pre-television family life. The fact remains that regardless of which of these images one subscribes to, the impact of television on the family has been substantial. A simple look at how the post-television family spends its time underscores this point. For within a decade of the introduction of this new communications medium into the American home, the average family had started to spend more time watching television than in formal employment. The average child now spends more time watching television than he does in school. And only sleep, as a single activity, consumes more of the family's time than watching the TV set.[1]

More importantly, this substantial alteration in family time budgeting raises questions about corresponding changes in the underlying relationships of family life. At a minimum, activities which previously accounted for substantial portions of the family's time are now performed more efficiently or have been altered due to the presence of television.

What are some of these activities? A partial listing might be as follows:

—interaction within the family (supervising children, family recreation, etc.)

—interaction with relatives and neighbors

—formal employment

—involvement in activities beyond the neighborhood (social, occupational, civic, etc.)

—housekeeping (cleaning, shopping, supervising children, repairing, etc.) and self-maintenance activities (eating, sleeping, etc.)

—individual leisure activities (reading, other media, recreation, etc.)

—"free" time (random wandering, sitting on the porch, daydreaming, etc.)

These are not meant to be exclusive categories. For example, as extended families become more separated by distance, "interaction with relatives" becomes synonymous with "activities beyond the neighborhood." Similarly, leisure activities which previously took the individual or family out of the home, such as movie-going or spectator sports, can now be consumed directly in the home.

But again, the point that emerges is that household acceptance of television (along with that of other home appliances, including the automobile and the telephone) reflects changes in the balance of family activities, the place and manner in which these activities are carried out, and the degree to which family interdependence has been sustained or reduced. The mother's housekeeping activities, for example, which used to occur in isolation or were accompanied by "small talk" with grandmother (who lived in the same house) or with the next-door neighbor, are now likely to be accompanied by the one-way "small talk" of a morning TV show (e.g., *Dinah's Place, Not for Women Only,* or *Password*) or an afternoon soap opera. [2] These changes in how housewives are spending their time may in turn lead to more basic alterations of the woman's relationship to the home and family life. [3]

The availability of television has undoubtedly also altered the wife's relationship to the husband (and vice versa). I am not referring here to the images of husband-wife relationships that television projects but to the time in the husband's life that television takes up. This is important from the point of view of family structure, since the husband is probably spending more time within the home now than at any time within the last two hundred years. This could well be an underlying factor in the mounting pressure to re-examine the basic husband-wife relationship. [4]

Socialization of the Young

The relation of television to child care activities within the home is also interesting to explore. In fact, this subject has been overlooked even as increasing attention has been placed on the effect of specific types of television programs on children. Will violence in television cartoons produce violence-prone children and adults? Do TV ads for children's toys create harmful or unnecessary consumer pressures? Is *Sesame Street*'s impact on reading long-term or short-term? These are questions well worth examining, but not at the expense of understanding the overall impact of television on child-adult relationships within the family unit.

How have these relationships been affected? To begin with, it can be argued that television has been substituted for one of the basic functions of the extended family, namely, the assistance that has traditionally been provided by the grandmother (or grandfather, or aunt, or uncle) in caring for the very young. To be sure, there are other factors responsible for the declining role of the extended family, ranging from the increasing availability of retirement benefits to the fact that fewer children are being raised by the American family. Yet the role of television in this regard may also be significant. Except in cases where both parents are engaged in formal employment, the TV set can usually provide the day-care assistance that used to be fulfilled by the presence of a third adult in the family. Now it is only in special instances, when both parents want to go out in the evening, for example, that such a presence is required.

Television's role in the socialization of the young also needs to be highlighted. The trend away from direct parental involvement in the socialization of children is not a new one. Both the increasing separation of home and work place and the increasing formalization of schooling have served to limit parental supervision of the social and emotional development of the young. Television, however, has reinforced this tendency. For now even those limited moments when parent and child are both together in the home are subject to the competitive appeal of the TV set (or radio, or record player, or telephone). At the same time, television programming is shaping the child's attitudes toward work situations, consumption, politics, love, and family life itself.

Moreover, the parent's ability to control the content of the TV fare on which children are brought up is even more removed than his or her control over school curriculum, where at least some form of indirect control can be exercised either informally through parent-teacher meetings or formally through community decisions on school expenditures. The only recourse in the case of television is to turn off the set selectively. Yet this requires careful monitoring of programming (which is subject to more change than the primary or secondary school curriculum) as well as the ability to provide alternative child-oriented activities, which has been lessened by the demise of the extended family.

That television has not had a more disruptive effect on parent-child relationships may be due to the fact that parents watch many of the same programs (or types of programs) as their children and are therefore exposed to the same values, attitudes, and role models. Consequently, a television-based form of family integration is maintained. Whether such integration will prevail with the growth of multiple-set households and the advent of multi-channel cable TV systems is a question that is well worth asking. [5]

The Urban Environment

Television has contributed not only to changes in the internal structure of the family but also to the relationship of the household to the broader community. In conjunction with the automobile, the advent of television, the telephone and other media has led to the superimposition of a new mobility-based community environment on the proximity-determined neighborhood of former years. Through time, the members of the family have come to depend less and less on the neighborhood to support their various activities. They have withdrawn from the local bar, grocery store, social club, movie theater, or sewing circle in favor of national brand-name products (sold in supermarkets and advertised on television), nighttime TV entertainment from New York and California (or, alternatively, recreational spots located outside the neighborhood, whether municipal parks or ski resorts), and social contacts at the metropolitan (rather than neighborhood) scale.

Layer by layer the functional and symbolic meaning of the neighborhood has been unpeeled. First, its economic function was relegated to the specialized employment or shopping center. Next, its social and recreational role was taken over by either home-based television and radio or specialized recreational facilities further away. Now, even the neighborhood's traditional function in providing physical security is being challenged by television's impact on our use of time and space and on our perception of public safety. As a recent study indicates, viewers of television, in particular heavy viewers, overestimate the occurrence of violence and street crime.[6]

More specifically, our decreased use of neighborhood streets—except as thoroughfares for the automobile—has undermined their ability to provide physical security. Today's common notion of public safety stops at the shell of the individual dwelling unit, which we attempt to safeguard by means of multiple door locks, handguns in the night table, intricate security alarms, and high-rise buildings. What happens in the streets, as the Kitty Genovese incident so dramatically illustrated, is of no direct concern. Our perception of personal security is largely determined by the crime reports of the daily news show or the cops and robbers serial dramas. Along with recreation and marketing, security has been nationalized.[7]

What has been the impact of this emerging electronic community on our urban environment? On the one hand it has facilitated the attainment of material values and comforts. More and more families have been able to set up households in the suburbs, where land is more plentiful, without losing their connectivity to economic, social and cultural amenities. In the future, social connectivity and household comfort may be even more favorably combined in the New Rural Society that Peter Goldmark has projected, where access to urban amenities will be guaranteed by advanced communications technology in a context of low-density habitation and ecological balance.[8]

But, on the other hand, our initial encounter with the electronic community has also raised a host of issues concerning the state of the urban community. The opportunities of the detached but plugged-in household are being weighed against the physical, social and economic dislocations that have taken place. Highways uprooting families have been built; our ability to evaluate consumer products and political candidates has been reduced; collective neighborhood activities and spaces have been undermined.[9]

In sum, the impact of television on community life has been significant, particularly if seen as part of a larger technological transformation of the urban environment. Urban space has been extended but also fractured. As a result, efforts aimed at reconstituting a sense of community are being undertaken with renewed passion, as evidenced by recent pressures for neighborhood control, historical preservation, highway stoppages, and the return to a "village" scale in urban architecture. To what extent television's future development will hinder or facilitate such efforts is a question that television viewers and critics can no longer afford to ignore.

Tomorrow's Electronic Community

The last area of social and economic activity that the local neighborhood continues to dominate is the provision of community services. For most households it remains the locus of the school, the police and the fire precinct, the access road, and the garbage pickup. In some instances it is still the place where commercial and professional services are provided—for instance, banking, newspaper delivery, shopping, and medical services. But it is also this area of community services that is being prospected by the proponents of the new communications technologies. As television matures into the home communications center of tomorrow, they argue, it will be able to deliver many of these same services directly to the home.

How will this extension of television's traditional powers occur? From a technological point of view, this question can be answered in a relatively straightforward manner. (The answer in terms of social impact is, as I will suggest further below, more complicated.) In essence, the new communications media will extend television's capabilities in the following ways:

(1) *Channel Abundance:* Today's cable television systems are mandated by FCC regulation to carry 20 television channels. Some systems already have the capability to transmit over 30 channels, and more could be added in the future if needed. The point is that it is now possible to transmit more television to the home than simply by the over-the-air channels that are available in a given locality. Viewers can become more selective about when or what they watch.

(2) *Audience Divisibility:* Programmers can also be more selective about who they reach. Through multiple head ends or special converter and scrambler devices, and ultimately through computer addressing of programs, programmers will be able to pinpoint the specific audience (by income, ethnicity, neighborhood, special interests, etc.) that they are most interested in reaching. Early forms of this capability are currently in operation in pay television experiments, medical programming for physicians, and local-origin programs that are aimed at a specific community rather than an entire metropolitan area.

(3) *Display Alternatives:* Programmers will not be limited to transmitting video messages alone. The augmented television terminals of tomorrow will be capable of receiving a variety of data, sound, and video messages, including stop-frame displays of print, facsimile, stereo sound, and large-screen television. Various hybrid communication forms will undoubtedly emerge, involving simultaneously or in sequence still pictures, moving images, captions, textual printouts, or supplementary sound tracks.

(4) *Feedback Mechanisms:* Some of the home devices will allow for inputs as well as outputs. The consumer or a surrogate (e.g., his electricity meter or

home burglar alarm) will be able to send messages back to the programming source, eliciting particular programs, registering opinions, or responding to questions regarding his banking transactions, shoppping needs, or knowledge of early American history. Home response mechanisms are likely to be limited to data and possibly voice communication. However, full-scale two-way video conferences may also be feasible on a limited basis, for example, between business or institutions.

(5) *Storage Capability:* Finally, both programmer and viewer will have access to increased storage capability. Data banks tied to the programmer will monitor and record various transactions between the viewer and the programmer, storing these for future reference. The viewer, on the other hand, will be able to record television programs on video cassettes (or to acquire them directly in that form) for playback at a convenient time. In fact, repeated and selective playback will be possible, as a result of which television will function more like the audio record or the book and less like a mass broadcasting system.

These are some of the capabilities that will be introduced by the new communications media, in particular by cable communications and a variety of ancillary technological developments. All of these capabilities are available in the laboratory today, and most of them are already being tested in selected areas. The questions that remain are how rapidly will these developments permeate our society and how desirable are they? What is no longer uncertain, however, is that in the future, whether five or ten or fifteen years from now, television will affect virtually all aspects of our daily lives.

The days of television as a spectator activity, during which we passively witness the unfolding of a Sunday afternoon football game, a light comedy serial, a Geritol psychodrama, or a national political convention, will be replaced by a television through which we directly engage in the act of learning, shopping, voting, and working.

Learning from the Home

The image of tomorrow's communications-supported home learning facility that is usually presented in graphic or film simulations is that of a child sitting in front of a video display console with his or her hands on an adjacent keyboard. At times the picture is that of an adult, since presumably the console will also be used for learning practical information such as how to repair the plumbing or how to plant tomatoes, as well as for continuing formal education. In the film simulations there are usually some shots of the actual operation of the console, showing how the student can interact with computer-generated questions, can retrieve factual data or images on demand, or can even create animated designs on the console. Interactive home learning, in short, will be to *Sesame Street* what the dual-mode guideway (the Ford Motor Company's most advanced concept in "people-moving") is to the Model T.

It is reasonable to assume that our learning ability will be enhanced by the availability of such a home learning facility. For example, curriculum choice will be expanded, since the user will have access to a considerably wider array of programming than is true in the typical school today. Self-pacing in instruction will become more possible in that the user will not have to adjust to the pace that is set in a conventional classroom. And the new facility will presumably be free of the human-relations biases that can exist in the traditional teacher-student relationship, whether due to race, sex, ethnic differences, or personality characteristics.

But the notion of a home learning facility also raises some difficult questions. How will this new communications medium affect educational objectives that have little to do with factual learning? It is not likely to provide day-care or socialization experiences, for example. Will it be responsive to the communications differences of different groups, as defined by age, ethnicity, or cognitive proficiency? In reducing social bias will it also reduce effective contact and comprehension? Will interactive home learning reduce our ability to deal with everyday problem situations due to its inherent abstraction of the learning process? Even though televised and computer-assisted forms of instruction have proven to be effective learning tools in the past, we have little knowledge of their impact on overall learning and problem-solving capabilities at the point that these tools become dominant (rather than occasional) learning modes.

Shopping from the Home

Considerable divergence of opinion exists concerning how "home shopping" will actually operate, even among the early promoters of this particular communications service. The more rudimentary proposals call for the consumer to push a single button at the end of a commercial, thereby indicating a desire to purchase the product. Alternatively, special shows may be produced to exhibit a department store's or supermarket's wares, during which viewers will be able to ask questions concerning particular items. Or, in still another rendition, the remote purchasing process is compared to computer-assisted instruction, where the consumer will be able to ask for information on a class of commodities (e.g., rental housing, automobiles, clothing, used furniture, etc.) and then through a series of branching routines be able to determine the product that meets his or her specific needs.[10]

It is also unclear how the product will be delivered once the electronic purchase is made. It is unlikely that a slow delivery process of the kind that is available today through mail-order catalogues will be sufficient to launch this new communications service. In fact, a whole host of delivery, warehousing, and managerial questions arise as one begins to contemplate seriously the establishment of remote shopping on a widespread basis. The electronic ordering mechanism, it turns out, is only a small part of the home shopping "system" that will be required. (The same can be said for other home communications services, whether remote burglar alarms, facsimile services, or medical care.) After all, the retailing trend for the past three decades has been away from home delivery and the corner store to much more centralized outlets such as supermarkets and regional shopping centers. Reversing this pattern will take more than an electronic push-button device.

But overlooking for the moment these practical problems, the appeal of an instantaneous home shopping facility, given the decline of neighborhood shopping, remains nonetheless considerable. Added choice, greater consumer information, convenience, and perhaps even cost savings due to sales economies are values that could conceivably be gained through home shopping. From a social viewpoint, the resulting decrease in shopping trips could help reduce air pollution and energy consumption. And access to commodities, which continues to be a problem in rural areas as well as inner-city poverty areas, could be equalized.

These are some of the potentially positive benefits. At the same time, less desirable social and economic consequences could also occur. For example, shopping trips today retain a quasi-social character. Even if market bartering and social discussions with the grocer are disappearing phenomena, shopping still involves a degree of social contact; at a minimum, it is a change of pace in day-to-day routine activity. As it is turned into a mechanized decision function, this may reduce social involvement and increase alienation.[11] Similarly, the economic base of the local pharmacy, the specialty shop, or the downtown department store may be undermined, leaving us wtih unexciting cities and further disrupting the urban economy and related social structure.[12]

Voting from the Home

An alteration of our political system is also likely to occur in tomorrow's electronic community. Channel abundance will allow the home viewer to follow local town council or PTA proceedings. Feedback mechanisms will permit him to register an opinion at these proceedings or to vote in national referenda. And access to stored information will facilitate the collection of facts about candidates, agencies, and issues. As a result of these developments, the mutual cynicism that so often distorts relationships between citizens and government officials could be reduced through a more continuous information flow.

But once again the underlying impact of these technological

capabilities is more difficult to pinpoint. Will access to the political system be truly broadened or will new entry requirements be placed on such access? One problem is that the ability to interact effortlessly by means of a remote communications device may not be universal.[13] The costs of such a home voting service, unless covered by the government, could also restrict participation, thereby creating a new kind of second-class citizenship. And the feedback mechanisms might be centrally controlled, so that instead of fostering genuine participation and the raising of issues the voter's response would be limited to pre-structured agenda items and choices.

Both the effectiveness and impact of home voting systems will, in other words, depend on how these are actually designed and implemented. The inclination at present is to visualize them as conveyors of instantaneous national referenda. Yet there is some question whether the lack of such electronic plebiscites is a root problem of contemporary American democracy. Would having a national election every month or every week to contend with the latest political crisis improve the system or simply multiply its current deficiencies? Would it not be more fruitful to expand participation in the political resolution of more specialized issues, whether the problems of the handicapped, foreign import quotas, or airport expansion? This, however, may run counter to the incentives underlying "digital democracy," namely, to raise issues in which the largest number of individuals will want to participate. The old television economics of appealing to the widest audience may survive the new television technology.

Working from the Home

Once we develop the technological capability and the psychological willingness to learn, shop, and engage in politics by remote interactive communications, the final step will be to connect the home to the work place. This will permit many of us to work at home, accessing files, secretaries, and corporate managers by means of remote communications devices. Since white-collar workers (the expanding sector of the economy) already spend much or perhaps most of their time in data-processing and communications activities, the notion of performing these same jobs on a highly decentralized basis is not necessarily utopian. Moreover, the ramifications on the tangle of social problems that are generated by daily commutation to work—that is, traffic congestion, air pollution, and energy consumption—could be very positive if home-bound work were to become an accepted practice.[14] At a minimum, work might be decentralized to a more local level, thereby cutting down on the length of the average commutation trip.[15]

This vision of "communicating to work," as Peter Goldmark has called it, is appealing both to the social planner and to the suburban employee faced with an hour-long drive two times each working day. But again a number of issues need to be examined before this new form of employment can be generally prescribed. There are several practical concerns. Can the variety of communications tasks involved in the business world be converted to a remote communications mode? Some, of course, have already been converted to the long-distance telephone, remote facsimile, or on-line computer services. And the new technologies, such as two-way video conferences, will allow even more business functions to be handled on a remote basis. Still the suspicion remains that certain intricate business activities, in particular negotiations that precede major decision-making, require face-to-face contact. More importantly, such contact may be essential to the maintenance of corporate morale and as a stimulant to other employment functions.

The notion of home-based work also raises important social and psychological issues. At present the ritual of departing the home for work is a deeply-imbedded concept that governs the daily behavior of most workers. The physical separation of home and work place underlies our economic and cultural behavior. How readily can these habits be changed? Do we, as a society, want to change them? And what will happen to family life when formal work invades the private household?[16]

What generalizations can be drawn from this discussion of four separate dimensions of tomorrow's electronic community? One, at least, is that the electronic community will not be a steady utopian (or counter-utopian) state in which society and culture are transformed once and for all. Rather it will be an evolving social process, during which the practical and economic difficulties of engaging in fundamental community activities on a remote basis will be worked out through trial and error, one at a time.

Similarly, the social impact of the new communications tools that are brought into being will not always be rapidly detectable, but over time, combined with other societal developments, they could be profound. The home, for example, is likely to become an even more intensive center for activity than it is today, but whether it will gain or lose in intimacy as a result remains to be seen. The work place may become less dependent on the economies of agglomeration that sustain today's cities and will be free to locate its various functions in different locations (including the home). But this may exacerbate rather than resolve the social problems of the metropolis. And in general our contact universes, whether shopping, learning, or work-related, will probably be expanded. In another sense, however, they may be collapsed, in that the time we will be able to accord to any one contact will be considerably shortened.

In sum, it will be the manner in which the new technologies are introduced and implemented that will determine their ultimate impact. This realization places a major responsibility on individuals and organizations involved in the design, marketing, and regulation of communications innovations. It also calls for the emergence of a new kind of television criticism, which, as I will argue at the end of this essay, must begin to examine the overall television environment that is being produced and not only individual programs. For in the future television's role as a monolithic entertainment medium will be fragmented by the advent of the new technologies, much as our cities have been dispersed through suburbanization.

The Future of Television

Like the telephone and radio which preceded it, television began as a relatively aimless technical invention and as a luxury consumer commodity. It had no content to speak of. Then gradually, borrowing heavily in production techniques and programming concepts from media predecessors, it emerged into a mass-entertainment medium. This, to a large extent, is the television we watch today: part radio, part cinema, part theater, and part athletic event.

But even in establishing its identity as an entertainment medium, the roots of a more variegated communications medium were beginning to take hold. The TV box began to carry marketing messages, newscasts, educational programs, and morning and evening talk shows. It became a purveyor of social roles, attitudes, and information, as well as entertainment. Even the serials convey not only emotions and cartharsis but specific images of how social roles can interact, how products satisfy, how institutions operate, and how values are fulfilled. These images have become as much a part of American reality as highways or frozen foods.

In short, television has already passed through several phases of transformation and is likely to continue doing so. It has become a complex social innovation, one that cannot be defined solely by its technical parameters, or by static concepts of economic demand. Both old and new technical properties of television interact with changes in buiness markets, government decisions, and social or cultural needs and preferences.

And the medium will continue to evolve in the future. But in what ways? How will the transition from today's mass medium to tomorrow's electronic community be accomplished?

Television as a Selective Medium

One way in which television will evolve—and is, in fact, already evolving—is in the direction of more "selective" communications services. It should be noted in this regard that television viewing patterns have changed considerably over the past ten years. The typical household no longer has only one TV set. Various economic factors have encouraged this new multiple-set household to come into being, including increased discretionary income, the reduction in the price of TV sets, and the availability of color television. At the same time the more individualistic viewing pattern that has resulted has been caused by, and has as well contributed to, several larger social transformations, including the disappearance of traditional local forms of recreation (e.g., bars, neighborhood theaters, social clubs) and the fragmentation of entertainment and information pursuits within the family.

If these trends persist, television is likely to become an increasingly selective medium. While the members of the family household may continue to watch certain programs jointly, an increasing portion of their viewing time will be consumed on an individual basis in a manner consistent with their different schedules, tastes, and information needs. Selectivity, in this sense, is also likely to mean diversity—not necessarily diversity as defined by traditional cultural critics, namely high-, middle- and low-brow programming, but diversity of the following kinds:

(1) time diversity (i.e., the same program made available at different times of the day, week or year in response to the fluctuating demand and convenience of viewers)

(2) programming diversity (i.e., greater variety in sports or movie programming, talk shows, news, children's programming, etc.)

(3) functional diversity (i.e., availability of programs not only for entertainment but for other uses as well, whether self-education, hobbies, shopping, specialized information, etc.)

The advent of multi-channel cable television and of pay television will reinforce this trend, already apparent at the margins of broadcast television (i.e, UHF stations, morning and late-evening programs, etc.), toward a more selective utilization of the medium. The viewer of tomorrow will have greater choice about when a program can be viewed, what that program is, and the manner in which television can be responsive to his or her needs. Cultural, educational, and other forms of nonentertainment programming will begin to flourish.

At the same time, the fragmentation in television viewing resulting from this increased selectivity is likely to have social and cultural consequences. If viewers watch sports or local news instead of national news, this may affect our level of national integration, in which television as a mass medium has played a major role. If viewers are drawn more and more to programs that correspond to their minority tastes, whether cultural, ethnic, or life-style related, this may create social, economic and possibly political tensions. And if within a given household TV viewing becomes highly individualistic, the nuclear family will experience further strains, leading possibly to a transformation of its current functions.[17]

Television as a Service Medium

It is the functional diversification of television that will produce the most obvious changes in the utilization of the medium. Up to the present our common notion of television has been that of a medium which has little bearing on ordinary, day-to-day life. It has been there to amuse and entertain us after a heavy day's work; to take us away from the boredom or frustration of daily housekeeping; to report on distant political events at City Hall, Washington, or Peking; or to enlighten us occasionally through cultural programming. Compared to the telephone, or even the daily newspaper, television's relation to our daily lives has been negligible.

Increasingly, however, television will begin to enter the daily activity patterns of our seasonal and life-cycle existence. It will cease to play solely a mythical, expressive, or cathartic role and will become an instrumental medium, helping us to learn, to shop, to make business decisions, and to engage in active leisure and community pursuits. In fact, the general lessening of distinctions between work and play, public and private space, and family and collective spheres will be reflected in tomorrow's "service video." We will tune in to get advice from a doctor, to find out how to fill out IRS forms, to learn how to play tennis or a musical instrument, to upgrade occupational skills, or to participate in a local zoning decision.

Another type of television diversity will accompany this evolution—*space* diversity. The selective use of television will not only expand in the home but also in other places, such as schools, hotels, hospitals, retail outlets, and workplaces. These will not be entirely new uses of television, since the medium has been utilized on a closed-circuit basis for educational, training, marketing and other purposes for the past two decades. But these specialized uses will become more commonplace. Moreover, the conceptual distinction between, for example, television used for monitoring purposes in a bank and television as a mass entertainment vehicle is likely to disappear. What will emerge instead is a notion of the spectrum of uses to which television can be put, some serving very specialized or local purposes, others involving widely dispersed but still selective audiences, and still others encompassing truly mass audiences.[18]

Television as a Hybrid Medium

As it becomes more of a service medium, television will also become more of a hybrid medium. To begin with, the imaginary line that has traditionally been drawn between video and print and that is only transgressed by television when production credits are shown will be gradually eliminated. This will occur not so much because of a direct infusion of print into the TV medium but because of the emerging relationship between television and the computer. Computer-assisted instruction, for example, has always depended on the digitalized transmission of textual content to a cathode ray tube or other visual display device. It is this type of communications capability that is being incorporated into the interactive television experiments that are currently being launched.[19]

The relationship with print will be reinforced in other ways as well. For example, Caravatte-Kleiman, "a video publishing" firm, recently produced a video cassette that is indexed like a book. Utilizing a video cassette machine, the viewer can go forward to those segments (pages) that are of relevance to an immediate information need. The program can be "read" selectively or "re-read" like a book. Can "speed viewing" be far behind? Another example of media hybridization, involving television, print, and the telephone, is the video reference service currently offered by the public library in Casper, Wyoming. A cable television subscriber can call up the library by phone, request the display of a textual or graphic item (e.g., menus, statistics, maps), and view it over a television channel in his home.

The matrix of possible relationships between television on the one hand and the computer and printed, graphic, and other audio forms of communications on the other, is virtually infinite. This is particularly true as television ceases to be simply a reception medium and becomes a storage, recording, and interactive tool as well. The systematic exploration of this matrix will lead to many discoveries which at present are hardly conceivable. It will also raise new questions concerning "man-machine interaction" and the social and psychological impact of these new communications forms, not all of which will be equally accessible or equally manageable for the average home viewer. Technical proficiency, or media literacy, may limit the service benefits that tomorrow's television can provide us.

Television as an Active Medium

How will the gap between today's passive consumer of television and the active participant of tomorrow be breached? This, ultimately, may be the overriding issue that determines the character of tomorrow's electronic community. Today our ability to utilize television in an active mode is analogous to our ability to explore the moon. We are at the point of departure, but only a very few individuals have passed through the elaborate training exercises required to perform the task—and even they must contend with biological, technological, and environmental barriers to achieve free movement on the lunar landscape. Our ability to actively explore the television medium is similarly constrained.

In part, the problem lies with our overall ability to utilize technology and, more specifically, communications media. Apart from voice, ball-point, and camera, the active utilization of communications media is, as a rule, reserved for specialists. Most of us, even today, cannot type. Many telephone users have never called the operator for information. Most of us are frustrated by the UHF dial on our TV sets. And most of us have never made a film, a videotape, or even an audio cassette recording. The prospects for a society where active media utilization is the norm are not high. Technical, psychological and economic barriers stand in the way.

Fortunately, the first signs of the active utilization of television are increasingly evident. The availability of low-cost portable television recording equipment, and the FCC requirement that all cable television systems provide free "public access" time to an individual or organization that requests it, are particularly significant developments in this regard. Most large cities now have one or more community video centers where the making of videotapes by individuals, whether community organizers, artists, or senior citizens, is encouraged and facilitated. And video training and tape exchange programs are being organized by schools, libraries, museums, church groups, and other community institutions.[20]

Television as a Community Environment

As the time approaches when television will not only affect our spare time but our everyday activities, its significance as a communications medium will also change. Television will no longer be solely a purveyor of consumer products and social relaxation. More and more it will become a total communications environment, as complex and variegated as the offices, schools, department stores and neighborhood parks, where our social and economic activities take place today. Increasingly important portions of our community life will occur on television, through television, or as a result of television and the other emerging electronic media.

The electronic community that will be created will at times enhance community life as we know it today and at times undermine it; more often than not it will compete with it for our attention, our response, our resources and values. As we have already seen, television today is capable of heightening our concern about safety in the streets; tomorrow it may substitute for much of our need to use these streets as community spaces. Television has already started to short-circuit our schools and political institutions by creating a more palatable and accessible electronic medium for the consumption of educational and political imagery. Tomorrow it may replace these institutions by interactive, multi-media linkages between central data banks and dispersed subscribers. And, as Martin Pawley has recently suggested, it may lead to the further privatization of both family life and national identity.[21] The community of today may become a museum, a mere archaeological referent for new electronically-supported life-styles and social institutions.

The Luddites would, of course, prefer to shatter the electronic community before it is too late. The espousers of technological utopia see its arrival as a new level of human evolution. Both, however, recognize that the most phenomenal aspect of the electronic community is its developmental pace. In less than a quarter century its foundations have been ubiquitously laid throughout our society. In another quarter century it may become the predominant environment in which we live.

In short, the challenge of ensuring that the electronic community enhances the quality of life and encourages active and equitable involvement in this new community sphere cannot be underemphasized. Our recent experience with the physical and social environment in which we currently live has hopefully shattered our naiveté concerning how a convivial yet complex living environment is brought into being. The naiveté of the business firm that claims it is only adding a new product or technology to the marketplace; the naiveté of government that formulates its policies in response to short-term political pressures rather than long-range communications priorities; the naiveté of the systems planner or engineer who believes that a neatly-drawn blueprint can anticipate the needs of a dynamic, pluralistic society; and the naiveté of the citizen who leaves decision-making about the future up to others until that future impinges on his doorstep: these are not adequate postures for the building of a new communications environment.

Television and the Critic

Fortunately, the deflation of naiveté has been one of the principal roles of the social critic. Clearly, the participation of such a critic will be crucial to the evolution of the electronic community, whose fabric remains to be determined by the numerous decisions that will guide and develop emerging communications technology. The problem that remains is that today's social critic may not be adequately prepared to take on this challenge.

Today's serious television critic generally falls in the tradition of the theater critic. He analyzes the thematic, aesthetic, or production values of a given event, that is, the single program or, at most, a series of programs. He is not likely to question the overall, environmental impact of television. By comparison, the journalistic critic may look beyond the values or effects of the latest TV special by examining the broader function of the media or by exposing the viewer (or reader) to the intricacies of judicial cases or federal regulations. But he is no more likely to probe into the subtle relationships that link technology, economics, and social change. Moreover, given the competitive tension between established media and emerging ones, he may be constrained in publicizing the advent of new communications services. [22]

Finally, the environmental critic, focusing on architecture, urban affairs, or the visual arts, may feel a distinct obligation to pursue the impact issues associated with high-rise projects, new highways and airports, or outdoor recreational programs. But ironically, television, because of the division of labor, has not been placed under his purview. Nor is it clear that the environmental critic could easily contend with the environmental impact of television, even if given the opportunity. The fact that television may shape the physical form of cities, family life, leisure activities, and political and social attitudes does not correspond to the prevailing concept of environmental influences.

In short, there is need for a new kind of television critic, one who will explore the broader impact of tomorrow's television but who will also be familiar with the regulatory and production constraints that define the medium today. The role of this critic will be to follow technological developments as much as programming events; to ensure that the results of scientific research on the effects of television and of field and laboratory experiments with the new technology are widely disseminated and understood; and to report on policy, business and educational deliberations on how the new media can be utilized and developed. Most importantly, it will be to stimulate us into deciding what kind of electronic community we want to live in—before technology decides for us.

Footnotes

1.   *Certainly, sitting on the front porch has been eliminated as a favorite family pastime. See Andrew H. Malcolm, "The American Front Porch Following the Rumble Seat into Oblivion,"* The New York Times, *August 11, 1974.*

2.   *This so-called "small talk" in fact serves an important function in providing role models, attitudinal support and basic family security to the house-bound mother. This has certainly been the case in extended family arrangements, where the grandmother-mother relationship was central to what Michael Young and Peter Willmont call the "informal women's trade union" that supported this family life-style. For a fuller discussion of this point, see their recent book,* The Symmetrical Family *(New York: Pantheon Books, 1973), pp. 91-93 and ff. To what degree soap operas have been able to substitute for this previous relationship is an interesting question in the understanding of contemporary family dynamics.*

3.   *I have not been able to locate any quantitative studies that would indicate a decrease in time spent in interaction in the home between the housewife and adults other than the husband. However, a recent cross-national study poses some interesting comparisions. The results of a survey of 44 U.S. cities shows that on the average the non-employed woman spends 0.2 hours per day interacting with other adults in the home. By comparison, in cities where television viewing is about half as frequent as in the U.S., the same figure rises considerably. It is 0.5 hours in a Hungarian city surveyed, 1.4 in a corresponding Russian city, and 2.6 in Lima-Callao, Peru. See Alexander Szalai, ed.,* The Uses of Time *(The Hague: Mouton, 1972).*

4.   *For a useful theoretical discussion of the impact of technology on family life see Eugene Litwak, "Technological Innovation and Ideal Forms of Family Structure in an Industrial Democratic Society," in Reuben Hill and Rene König, eds,* Families in East and West *(Paris: Mouton, 1970), pp. 348-396.*

5.   *It is significant in this regard that debates over the impact of television on children have focused on programming that parents are not likely to watch themselves, whether Saturday morning cartoons, children's consumer ads, or instructional programs such as Sesame Street. In fact, children are likely to receive more of their socializing, in simple quantitative terms, from evening programs, which absorb more of their weekly TV viewing time than do the programs that are specifically aimed at children. Yet the viewing of adult programming by children does not seem to cause as much parental unease.*

6.   *This is one of the preliminary findings of an ongoing study of the cultural impact of television that is being carried out by George Gerbner and Larry P. Gross at the Annenberg School of Communications, University of Pennsylvania. See their "Violence Profile No. 6," December 1974.*

7.   *For an interesting discussion of how neighborhood security might be regained, see Oscar Newman,* Defensible Space: Crime Prevention through Urban Design *(New York: Collier Books, 1973). Curiously enough, one of the recommendations of this book is that closed-circuit television systems be utilized in high-rise buildings for security monitoring purposes. In this manner, television could be employed to faciliate contact with our immediate physical surroundings rather than reduce it.*

8.   *Goldmark's proposal for a telecommunications-supported rural community of the future was first presented in chapter four of* Communications Technology for Urban Improvement, *Committee on Telecommunications, National Academy of Engineering (Washington, D.C., 1971).*

9.   *It should be noted that I am not arguing that television has reduced interpersonal interaction or that it has eliminated collective activities (i.e. civic, social, cultural, etc.) but only that this interaction is occurring less frequently at the neighborhood level.*

10.   *See, for example, "Toward a Market Success for CAI—An Overview of the TICCIT Program," Mitre Corporation, (McLean, Va., 1971).*

11.   *In most occasions when I have presented the concept of home shopping to women's groups, the reaction has been negative. The need to examine the product and "to get out of the house" were among the reasons cited for hostility to the idea. I am not sure, however, whether women who are formally employed would react in the same way.*

12.   *Subtle family arrangements regarding who has access to credit and who is responsible for the procurement of food and household commodities could also be altered.*

13.   *"Man-machine interaction" problems could arise with respect to any of the home communications services. Many individuals find manipulating the UHF dial on TV sets difficult or bothersome; in comparison, the push-button consoles of tomorrow may be much more difficult to operate. For example, a major problem encountered in a recent home banking experiment was the difficulty individuals had in "talking to the computer" through push-button telephones. Since the experiment took place in Seattle, this problem presumably arose even in the case of technically-trained aerospace workers. (See "New Inventions and a First-of-a-Kind Service that Failed,"* The New York Times, *December 29, 1973). For a home voting service to be effective it would have to be mechanically manageable for a broad cross-section of the population.*

14.   *Automobile travel is the single biggest consumer of energy in our society as well as greatest source of air pollution, and commuting to work is in turn the most frequent reason why such travel is undertaken.*

15.   *I have projected the concept of decentralizing employment sites to neighborhood "service parks" in "Telecommunications for Future Human Settlements,"* Ekistics, *Vol. 35, No. 211, June 1973, pp. 329-336. However, I also questioned the inevitability of substituting telecommunications for transportation. In the past whenever two offices, cities or continents have been linked by communications technology, the effect has usually been an increase in travel rather than its reduction.*

16.   *The fact that learning, shopping, and political participation may also occur in the home of the future suggests that a new form of household congestion will arise even if the traffic congestion outside will have been eliminated. At a minimum, houses will have to be redesigned to accommodate this multiplicity of activities, each of which may require a different kind of psychological and physical space.*

17.   *It is worth emphasizing that changes in television will be only one factor in the tensions and demands with which national, community and family institutions will have to cope in the future. Nonetheless, tensions present due to other factors could be magnified by the viewing patterns that tomorrow's television reinforces. For example, with respect to the family, the availability of more sports, educational, hobby-related, women's and children's programming may reinforce the separation between the adult and child members of the family that is already apparent in some families, according to Young and Willmont. Consequently, their questions about the growth of*

non-family activities on children become more salient, given the
television viewing patterns that are being projected. Will tomorrow's
children, ask Young and Willmont, be "less subject to control at
home, less bound by old disciplines, more out of the thoughts of
parents whose attentions are engaged elsewhere, more emancipated,
expected to become little adults at an earlier age than they
were. . . .?", op. cit., p. 174.

18.   The Swiss communications scholar René Berger has referred to these
three dimensions of television as micro, meso, and macro television.
He presented these concepts at a conference on the future of television held at the Museum of Modern Art in New York in January,
1974.

19.   These experiments are being supported not only by private industry
but also by the National Science Foundation, which has recently
funded several demonstration projects to examine the use of two-
way cable television in the delivery of government services.

20.   Similarly, psychiatrists, architects, lawyers, and social workers are
experimenting with specialized uses of television that pertain directly to professional practice. For an overview of community and artistic innovations in video, see my previous Aspen Institute Program on
Communications and Society report, The Video Implosion: Models
for Reinventing Television, which includes a bibliography of related
publications.

21.   Martin Pawley, The Private Future (London: Thames and Hudson,
1973).

22.   For example, the coverage accorded to cable television by the broadcast media has not been exemplary when compared to the attention
placed on space, bio-medical, or computer technologies or
technology-related social issues such as automobile safety or water
pollution.

Appendix

Planning Meetings: Palo Alto—January, 1974
New York—February, 1974
Cambridge—February, 1974

Aspen Conference: August, 1974

ELIE ABEL
Dean
Columbia School of Journalism

RICHARD ADLER
Assistant Director
Aspen Institute Program on
    Communications and Society

JAMES ARMSEY
The Ford Foundation

RUDOLPH ARNHEIM
Psychology of Art
Harvard University

GENO BALLOTTI
Managing Editor
Daedalus

ERIK BARNOUW
Broadcasting historian

STEPHEN BENEDICT
The Rockefeller Brothers Fund

JAMES BILLINGTON
Woodrow Wilson Center
Smithsonian Institution

JULIUS BLOOM
Executive Director
Carnegie Hall Corporation

ASA BRIGGS
Vice Chancellor
University of Sussex

DOUGLASS CATER
Director
Aspen Institute Program on
    Communications and Society

GEORGE COMSTOCK
The Rand Corporation

DAVID CONNELL
Vice President
Children's Television Workshop

LAURENCE CREMIN
Teacher's College
Columbia University

MICHEL CROZIER
Center for Advanced Study in
    the Behavioral Sciences

DAVID DAVIS
The Ford Foundation

BENJAMIN DeMOTT
Department of English
Amherst College

NANCY DENNIS
Public Education Office
The Ford Foundation

ROGER FISHER
Harvard Law School

CHARLES FRANKEL
Department of Philosophy
Columbia University

LEWIS FREEDMAN
Producer
CBS

SAMUEL GIBBON
Graduate School of Education
Harvard University

STEPHEN GRAUBARD
Editor
Daedalus

HANS GUTH
Department of English
California State University,
    San Jose

PAUL HORGAN
Writer and historian

BRICE HOWARD
National Center for Experiments
in Television

SIDNEY HYMAN
University of Illinois,
Chicago Circle

KAS KALBA
Graduate School of Design
Harvard University

PAUL KAUFMAN
National Center for Experiments
in Television

JAMES KRAFT
Office of Planning and Analysis
National Endowment for the Humanities

GERALD LESSER
Graduate School of Education
Harvard University

DAVID LITTLEJOHN
School of Journalism
University of California, Berkeley

SAMUEL LUBELL
Author and political analyst

ROBERT MERTON
Center for Advanced Study
in the Behavioral Sciences

EDWARD P. MORGAN
ABC News

BILL MOYERS
Editor-in-Chief
Educational Broadcasting Corp.

ROBERT NORTHSHIELD
Executive Producer
NBC News

MICHAEL NOVAK
Associate Director for Humanities
The Rockefeller Foundation

JAKOB OETAMA
Editor-in-Chief
Kompas (Indonesia)

FATHER WALTER ONG
Center for Advanced Study
in the Behavioral Sciences

ITHIEL deSOLA POOL
Department of Political Science
Massachusetts Institute of
Technology

STEPHEN RABIN
Assistant Director, Media Program
National Endowment for the Humanities

MICHAEL ROBINSON
Department of Politics
Catholic University

DAVID ROTHMAN
Department of History
Columbia University

ROSITA SARNOFF
Managing Editor
The Video Publisher

DANIEL SCHORR
CBS News

ALBERTA SIEGEL
Department of Psychiatry
Stanford University

JOHN SISK
Department of English
Gonzaga University

DAVID SONTAG
Television producer

ISAAC STERN
Concert violinist

WARREN SUSMAN
Department of History
Rutgers University

JACK VALENTI
President
American Motion Picture Association

PAUL WEAVER
Associate Editor
Fortune Magazine

DAVID WEBSTER
Director-United States
British Broadcasting Corporation

HUW WHELDON
Managing Director of Television
British Broadcasting Corporation

RICHARD WILLIAMSON
Department of English
College of San Mateo

PETER WOOD
The Rockefeller Foundation

Communications Fellows and Program Staff

CHARLES CLIFT
School of Radio-Television
Ohio University

THOMAS CRONIN
Scholar-in-Residence
Aspen Institute

PAUL FITZPATRICK
University of Colorado

WILLIAM HARRIS
Massachusetts Institute of Technology

ANDREW MARGESON
Woodrow Wilson School
Princeton

MICHAEL NYHAN
Assistant Director
Aspen Institute Program on
    Communications and Society

Index